ACCESS 2003

MARK LEWIN

In easy steps is an imprint of Computer Step
Southfield Road . Southam
Warwickshire CV47 0FB . United Kingdom
www.ineasysteps.com

Notice of Liability
Every effort has been made to ensure that this book contains
accurate and current information. However, Computer Step and the
author shall not be liable for any loss or damage suffered by readers
as a result of any information contained herein.

Trademarks
Microsoft® and Windows® are registered trademarks of Microsoft
Corporation. All other trademarks are acknowledged as belonging to
their respective companies.

Printed and bound in the United Kingdom

ISBN 1-84078-272-2

Contents

Introduction to Access 2003

Access 2003 is a powerful, yet simple to use database package. This chapter explains what a database is and what features make Access so popular. You'll get a guided tour of the Access main screen; learn how to open and close an existing database and get help when you need it. We'll look at Microsoft's sample Northwind database which you can use to practise what you read in this book without worrying about damaging your own data. We'll also cover the main building blocks of an Access database: Tables, Queries, Forms and Reports.

Covers

Chapter One

What is a Database?

Definition

A database is an organized collection of information. Examples of databases include a telephone directory and a filing cabinet full of employee records.

The trouble with these databases is that their organization is inflexible. When you want to search for a specific item of information, your search needs to follow the ordering of the data. For instance, a TV Guide is a very simple example of a database, storing information about television programs organized by the date and time they are due to be broadcast. If you're looking for a particular program and you don't know when it's on then you'll have to start on day one and search systematically through all the entries for that day, from the earliest to the latest. If you don't find it there, you'll have to proceed to day two and continue your search until you either locate the program, or come to the end of the guide!

Wouldn't it be much simpler if you could sort the data, so that all programs were listed alphabetically by name? With a printed database like the TV Guide, the only way to do this is to grab your scissors and start cutting!

Computer Databases

Now consider a bank's database. This will likely contain records for hundreds of thousands of customers. Not just their contact details, but all the accounts they hold with the bank and the various transactions going through them. If a customer raises a query about one particular transaction then the bank's staff need to be able to locate it quickly. They will also want to select customers according to certain criteria for marketing purposes, offering them other products like loans and credit cards. Clearly a manual system would not be adequate for the bank's purpose and in fact banks use huge and sophisticated computer databases which allow them to locate individual transactions among millions within seconds. Today, when we talk about databases we are usually referring to databases held on computers. Because of their large storage capacities and ability to manipulate large amounts of data quicker than we could ever do manually, they are ideally suited to this task.

How Data is Stored

A computer database holds information in *tables*, which contain *records* comprised of *fields*.

If we used Access to create a TV Guide database, then the Scheduled Listings table might look like this:

The columns are the table's *fields*

	Program ID	Program Name	Program Type	Channel	Date	Time
	1	Pumpernickel Street	Childrens	Kidz	Monday	17:00
	2	Bridges Too Far	Movie	Family Faves	Wednesday	15:30
	3	The Pyramids	Education	Learning	Thursday	13:45
	4	George the Chipmunk	Childrens	Kidz	Thursday	15:00
	5	False Chances	Movie	Family Faves	Tuesday	22:00
	6	Billy and the Magic Bike	Childrens	Tots	Friday	09:00
	7	Majority Report	Movie	Matinee One	Wednesday	21:30

The rows are the table's *records*

Tables

A *table* is a collection of data about similar items. This table contains information about scheduled television programs.

Records

A *record* is the data pertaining to one particular item. This record contains information about the "False Chances" program.

Fields

A *field* is one specific piece of information about a record, in this case it's the Channel field, telling us that "False Chances" will be showing on the "Family Faves" channel.

Relationships Between Tables

Certain databases support the creation of logical links (or relationships) between the tables. This type of database is called a *relational database*. It enables information to be manipulated and presented to the user in many different ways without affecting the underlying data.

We'll learn about relational databases in the next topic.

Records are sometimes called "rows" or "observations". Fields are sometimes called "columns" or "variables".

What is a Relational Database?

A relational database system stores related data in separate tables. The bank for example, will keep customer contact information in one table and account and transaction data in others. By defining the *relationships* between these tables you can retrieve the data and use it for making queries and writing reports.

Data in a relational database can be sorted and the order of fields rearranged without affecting the actual data. Going back to our TV guide example, if the program details were stored in a relational database, we would be able to:

Search the **Program Type** field to see all the childrens' programs

Program Name	Program Type	Channel	Date	Time
▶ Pumpernickel Street	Childrens	Kidz	Monday	17:00
George the Chipmunk	Childrens	Kidz	Thursday	15:00
Billy and the Magic Bike	Childrens	Tots	Friday	09:00

Search the **Program Type** and **Date** fields to list all the movies showing on Wednesday

Program Name	Program Type	Channel	Date	Time
Bridges Too Far	Movie	Family Faves	Wednesday	15:30
Majority Report	Movie	Matinee One	Wednesday	21:30

Link to the **Actors** table, to see which actors starred in the film "Bridges Too Far"

Program Name	Actor Name
Bridges Too Far	Michael Douglas
Bridges Too Far	Charlie Sheen
Bridges Too Far	Cameron Diaz

A TV Guide is a trivial example. But in a database containing many thousands or even millions of records the ability to manipulate the data in this way is vital.

Why Use Microsoft Access?

Purists would argue that Access is not a relational database. Whether it is or not isn't important for our purposes, because Access includes many of the features found in "real" relational database packages at a fraction of their cost. And unlike most of them, the Access implementation is extremely easy to use.

Access is a simple yet sophisticated tool that makes storing, organizing and sharing your data a snap. Access lets you:

- Create sophisticated databases quickly

- Analyze and modify your data easily with queries

- Build forms which allow you to present your data in a format which is easy to read and allows for simple and accurate data entry

- Create elaborate reports from your data

- Present your data dynamically on the World Wide Web

- Share data with other Microsoft Office applications, such as Word (e.g. for mailing address details) and Excel (e.g. to make financial data available as a spreadsheet)

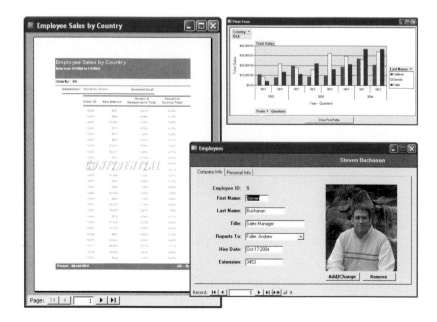

The Access 2003 Main Screen

Starting Access

Click on the **Start** button and point to **Programs** in the Start Menu, then click on Microsoft Access 2003 in the list of applications.

If you have used any of the other applications in the Microsoft Office suite, then this type of screen will look familiar. Access 2003 makes it easier than ever to find what you need, when you need it.

The Access Main Screen

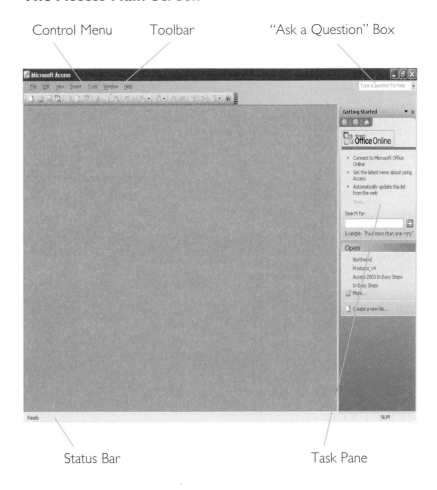

We'll now look at the components of the main screen.

The Control Menu

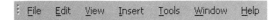

All the functions of Access can be found in one of the menus. For example, the File menu is where you open existing databases or create new ones and the View menu is where you adjust what you see on the screen.

The Toolbar

Hover the mouse over a button on the toolbar. After a second or two a little banner (known as a "tooltip") will appear which tells you what that button does.

The menu items you'll use most frequently have shortcuts in the Toolbar. You can choose which ones you see from the View menu's **Toolbars** option.

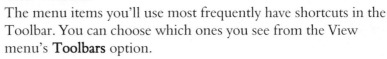

The Status Bar

The Status Bar gives you a running commentary on what Access is doing. When you first start Access it will say "Ready" because it's waiting for you to do something.

All these objects can be moved around the screen and "docked" along any side as required. To move an object, position the mouse pointer over the little dots on the left hand side until the cursor changes to a four-pointed arrow. Hold the left mouse button down and drag it to the desired position. Release the button to reposition the object.

Click here to switch between Task Panes

The Task Pane

Task Panes are designed to be there when you need them. The "Getting Started" Task Pane is there by default when you first start Access and others open automatically when you perform certain actions, such as creating a new database. On other occasions you will open them yourself, perhaps to get help (see p.14) or to search for a file (see p.18).

Getting Help with Access

Even expert Access users need help from time to time! Getting help in Access 2003 is easier than ever. If you're connected to the Internet, Access can also search Microsoft Office Online, giving you the most up-to-date information available.

There are three main ways of getting help in Access 2003:

- "Ask a Question"
- Use the Help menu
- Use the Help Task Pane

Ask a Question

1 Type your question in the box in the top right hand corner and hit the RETURN key

2 Access lists all the topics it thinks are relevant to your question. Click on a topic and …

3 Access gives you the information you need

4 Access can help you refine your search if necessary

Using the Help Menu and Help Task Pane

1 Click on **Microsoft Access Help** in the Help menu, or ...

2 ... select **Help** from the Task Pane menu

3 Type the query here and press the RETURN key

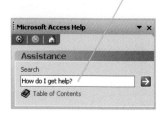

4 Click on a search result to find out more

Filtering Help

Sometimes you can get too much help! Use the filter options at the bottom of the Help Task Pane to be selective about what help you receive.

Use the "Search" box at the bottom of the Help Task Pane to expand or limit the scope of your search

Opening and Closing a Database

A standard Access database file has an MDB extension – e.g. TVGuide.mdb.

Access uses other extensions for particular types of file, such as Project files and Data Access Pages. Some of these we'll be covering in later chapters.

Browsing for an Existing Database

If you know what your database file is called and where to find it, you can locate and open it by one of the following methods:

- Select the **File > Open** menu option

- Click the **Open** icon on the toolbar

- Click the "More..." link on the **Getting Started** Task Pane

Use the Open File dialog box (pictured below) to navigate to your database file. Double click on the file to open it.

The Open File Dialog Box

Use these to navigate
to your database

Tools menu

You can open an Access database file anywhere within Windows, just by double-clicking it.

Click here for a list of databases you have opened recently

Click **Open** to open the highlighted database

You can choose which types of file appear in the list above here

Opening a Recent Database

Microsoft Access makes it easy to locate databases you have worked on recently, saving you the trouble of browsing for them. You can find a list of these:

at the bottom of the **File** menu ...

*If the list of recently used files isn't displayed in the File menu, click **Tools** > **Options**, then click the General tab and select the "Recently used file list" check box. You can also specify how many files it should show.*

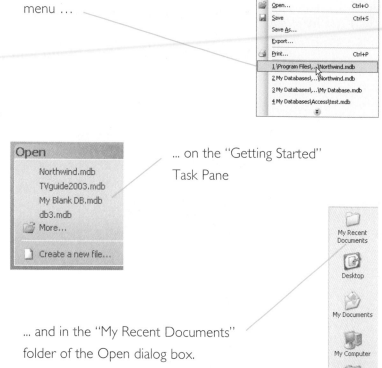

... on the "Getting Started" Task Pane

You can also find recently used files in Windows. Click the Start Button then Documents.

... and in the "My Recent Documents" folder of the Open dialog box.

Closing a Database

Close the database by either:

- Selecting the **File > Close** menu option

- Clicking the Access close button in the top right hand corner

- Clicking the Database Window Close button (which will close the database but keep Access open)

Searching for a Database

You can use Access to search for a database (or any other type of file) if you know its name, or part of it.

The best place to do this is from the Search Task Pane. Open the Search Task Pane by doing one of the following:

You can also search from the Open File dialog box Tools Menu (see p. 16)

- Select the **File > File Search** menu option

- Select it from the Task Pane Menu

Search Using the Help Menu and Help Task Pane

Enter the name (or part of the name) in the "Search text" box

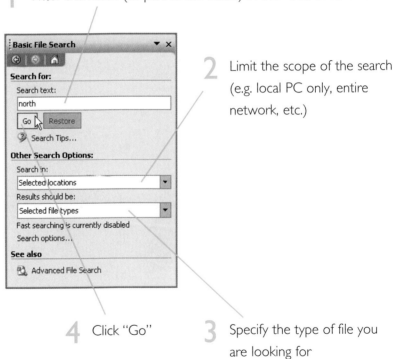

2 Limit the scope of the search (e.g. local PC only, entire network, etc.)

4 Click "Go"

3 Specify the type of file you are looking for

Consult Access Help for a detailed explanation of the advanced file search options.

Advanced File Searches

The Advanced File Search options allow you to narrow your search even further. Each file has certain properties you can search on, such as when the file was created, who created it and so on.

The Northwind Sample Database

Microsoft has usefully included a sample database in Access 2003.

The Northwind database is included as part of a typical install of Microsoft Office and can be found in the "Samples" folder beneath your Office directory.

Study the objects within the Northwind database to get an idea of what Access can do. Look at the design of the tables and the relationships between them to learn how to design your own databases.

This database contains examples of all the objects you'll find in a typical Access database as well as a number of more advanced features, like Data Access Pages. It's worth taking the time to experiment with the Northwind database, as doing so will teach you a great deal about database design as well as show you what Access 2003 is capable of.

Using the Northwind Database

1 When you open the Northwind database it fires up a splash screen. Click OK to proceed

2 The Switchboard form appears. This type of form merely acts as a "front end" to your database. We'll be learning how to create one in Chapter 10

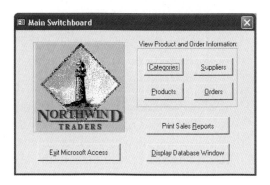

3 Have a look at the various forms and reports available from the switchboard and then click on the **Display Database Window** button to browse the underlying objects

The Database Window

Some databases don't lead you straight to the database window but take you straight into a switchboard form or splash screen instead. You can bypass either by holding down the Shift key when you click on the file to open the database.

If you're working with an object regularly, put it in a suitable folder in the Groups section. Right click on the object, click Add To Group and select the Group you wish to add it to. These don't have to be Access objects, they can be from any Office application. If you're regularly referring to a Word document for instance, you can put it here.

File Format: Microsoft has taken steps to ensure that you can use Access 2003 to work with databases created in older versions. The default file format is Access 2000 (and the Northwind database that ships with Access 2003 is still in 2000 format). When using the 2000 format, any functionality specific to versions 2002 or later is ignored. You can change the default file format by going to the Tools > Options > Advanced tab and changing the entry in the "Default File Format" drop-down.

When you open an Access database you are faced with the Database Window. This window is the control centre for your database and you'll be spending a lot of time here. Let's look at the components of the database window:

Open: view the existing object

Design: modify the highlighted object

New: create a new object of the type specified

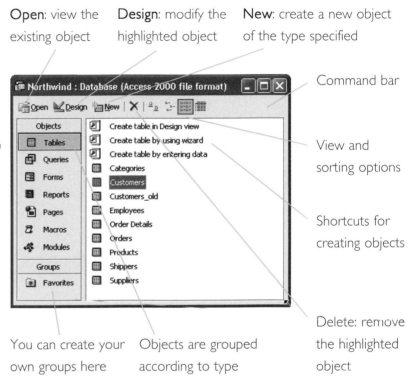

Command bar

View and sorting options

Shortcuts for creating objects

Delete: remove the highlighted object

You can create your own groups here

Objects are grouped according to type

Each page of objects has its own command bar with buttons relevant to that type of object. Some of these are common across all object types, such as the **Design** and **New** buttons. As well as a list of objects of a certain type, each page contains shortcuts to create new objects. For example, on the Tables page there are three shortcuts:

- Create table in Design View
- Create table using a wizard
- Create table by entering data

Database Objects

The core building blocks of most Access applications are Tables, Forms, Queries and Reports. To become proficient at Access you really need to know these well and we will be covering each in some depth in later chapters.

You can see all the objects in your database in the Database Window.

There are three other Access objects: Data Access Pages, Macros and Modules. Their use can make your database applications very sophisticated indeed and we will look at these too later on.

Tables

This is where your data is stored (as records) and is therefore the most important part of your Access database. All the other objects rely on the data in your tables to do their job. We are going to be covering tables in Chapter 3.

Forms

Forms are used mainly for data entry, or to display existing data in a user-friendly way. Although you can enter data in the Datasheet View, it's much better to have a form to guide you. With forms you can validate the data you enter and generally have more control over what ends up in your tables. Other uses for forms are as a dialog box to prompt the user for information or as a "switchboard", which we have already seen in the Northwind database (p. 19). See Chapter 6.

Queries

Queries allow you to manipulate the data in your tables. There are several different types and which one you use will depend on what exactly you are trying to do with your data. For instance, you would use a *select* query to create a subset of your data based on criteria you supply, specifying which fields you want to see and in what order the records should be sorted. You would use an *action* query to make bulk changes to your data, such as adding or deleting several records simultaneously. See Chapter 7.

Reports

Reports present the information in your tables in a polished format suitable for distribution. It's easy to create very sophisticated reports in Access that include totals, subtotals and graphs. Many of the concepts used in creating forms can be applied to building reports. See Chapter 8.

Pages

Data Access Pages are a type of web page specially designed for viewing information stored in your tables. Access makes it easy to display, share and update your data on the web. With data access pages you and other Access users in different locations can search, edit and add to a database solely from within your web browser and the web pages that represent your data will update dynamically as you do so. See Chapter 9.

Macros

Macros provide a means of automating tasks. As well as combining a number of operations in one easy step for convenience, you can also create macros that respond to certain events. For example, when the user presses a button you may wish to have the database close a form, or run a sequence of reports. See Chapter 10.

Modules

Modules are collections of program code written in *Visual Basic for Applications (VBA)*. VBA is suited for power users or software developers who require complete control over their applications. See Chapter 11. You might be feeling a bit apprehensive at the mere mention of programming, so let us put your mind at rest.

A Quick Note About Programming...

Why would you want to learn how to program? You don't have to learn how to program to get a great deal out of Access, but those who choose to, do so for one main reason: customization.

You don't need any programming skills to use Access. But once you see what you can achieve without knowing how to program, you may become curious about what else you could be capable of!

So why customize? Well, there are many reasons why you might want to customize your database applications. You can automate the most arduous tasks. Or you can create a more sophisticated user interface, minimize errors using more complicated validation checks and manipulate data at the touch of a button.

A detailed discussion on VBA programming is beyond the scope of this book but it is nevertheless well worth investigating. Newcomers to programming will find it a gentle introduction while old hands will find it a useful addition to their skills.

A short introduction to the subject is provided in Chapter 11.

Creating a Database

This chapter guides you through the creation of a new database. First, we'll look at some of the design decisions you'll need to make. Then we'll show you how to use the Database Wizard which makes it really easy to create databases based on pre-supplied templates. We'll finish by demonstrating how to create a new database from scratch.

Covers

Chapter Two

Database Design

Look at the Northwind database for a good example of database design.

Never rush blindly into creating a database without planning it first. Whole books could be (and have been) devoted to this subject, but we're going to give you a "crash course" in the basics in just a couple of pages!

Points to Consider When Creating a Database

- What do the users want the database to do?

- What tables are required to store the data?

- What fields are needed?

- How are the tables going to be related?

What Do the Users Want the Database to Do?

You need to understand exactly what your users want the database to be capable of. You need to know what sort of information you will be storing and how your users expect this to be surfaced – e.g. what forms and reports they require.

What Tables are Required to Store the Data?

The information in a single table should be limited to a single subject. For example you might have one table for employees and another for customers. This division of the data will enable you to maintain data in each table independently. You should also ensure that the data is not duplicated, so that each piece of information only needs to be updated in one place.

The Table Relationships diagram

For a quick glance at how your database is structured, look at the Table Relationships diagram, which you get to from the Tools > Relationships menu option.

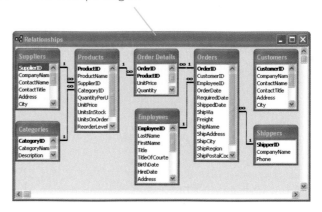

What Fields are Needed?

Never include any fields which duplicate information you already have.

When considering which fields are needed for each table it is important to avoid creating a field which could be derived from other fields. For example, in a Customer database you might have "Forename" and "Surname" fields, but it would be silly to have another field called "Fullname". Instead, you would use the information in the first two fields to get the Customer's full name.

Each record should have a field which uniquely identifies that record. This field is called the table's Primary Key.

The key icon by the "Customer ID" field signifies that this field is the Primary Key for the table

Field Name	Data Type
CustomerID	Text
CompanyName	Text
ContactName	Text
ContactTitle	Text
Address	Text
City	Text
Region	Text
PostalCode	Text
Country	Text
Phone	Text
Fax	Text

How Are The Tables Going to Be Related?

The relationships between the Tables is what gives Access its power, so it's important to get it right.

You'll need to decide how the tables are going to be related to one another. We're going to be covering Relationships in Chapter 4, but it is an important concept so it won't hurt to start thinking about it now.

To relate two tables, you use fields that are common to those two tables. Usually this is the Primary Key from the main table and what is known as the "Foreign Key" in the second table. To be related, the two fields need to share the same data type.

Relationships can be One-to-One, One-to-Many or Many-to-Many.

Using the Database Wizard

People often want databases for similar reasons, so Microsoft have included the Database Wizard. The wizard uses a number of templates to help you get started quickly.

1 Click the **New** button on the toolbar

The "New File" page appears on the task pane. As an exercise, we're going to create a Contact Management database.

2 Click the "On my computer" link

3 Select the **Databases** tab

4 Double-click on the Contact Management template

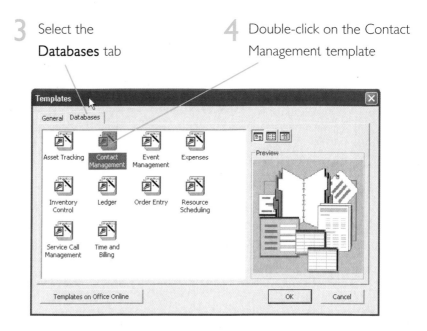

5 In the "File New Database" window give your database a name and save it

6 The Database Wizard starts.

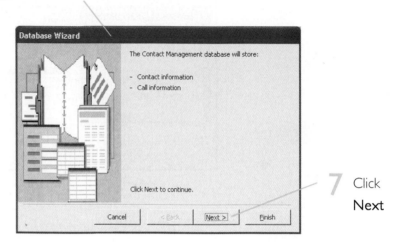

7 Click **Next**

8 These are the tables the wizard will create

9 Put a check next to a field to include it in your table

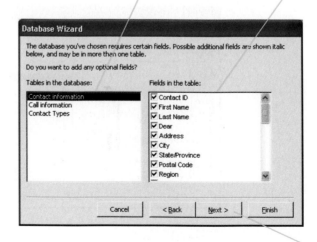

10 Click **Next**

|| Choose a style for the forms in your database

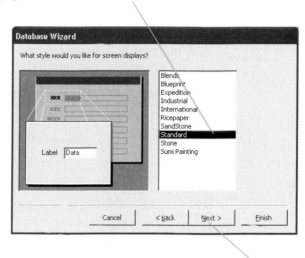

|2 Click **Next**

|3 Choose a style for the printed reports in your database

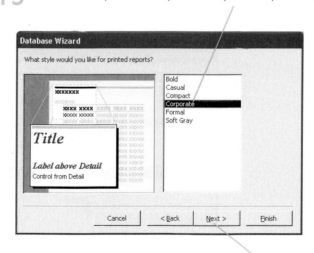

|4 Click **Next**

15 Give your
database
a name

16 If you want to include a
picture (optional), put a
check in the box

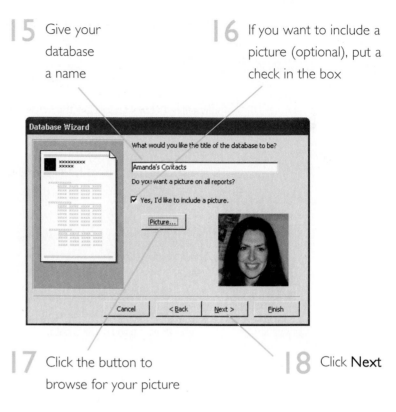

17 Click the button to
browse for your picture

18 Click **Next**

19 Click **Finish** on the next page of the wizard

20 Access creates your database ...

*The Database
Wizard doesn't
always give you
exactly what
you're looking for,
but it's a start. You can modify
the database in the Design View
later on.*

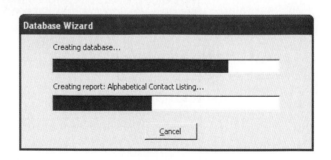

21 ... and launches your new database application

Creating a Database from Scratch

The Database Wizard is great if there's a template for the type of database you want to build. If there isn't one, you'll have to start from scratch.

If the prospect of creating an entire database from scratch is overwhelming, you can use the Database Wizard to get a head start and then modify the objects it has created for you.

1 Click the **New** button on the toolbar, or select the **File > New** menu option

2 Click on the "Blank Database..." link in the New File Task Pane

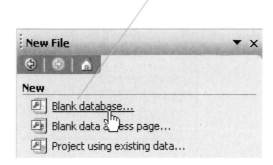

3 In the "File New Database" window, give it a name and save it

4 Access creates a blank database with the name you specify

This is just a blank database. In subsequent chapters we'll be showing you how to create the various objects that will allow your database to store, retrieve and display data.

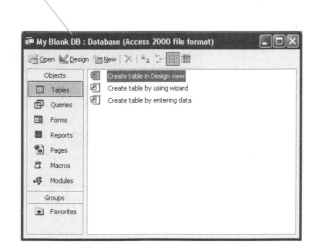

Tables and Fields

This chapter looks at the all-important tables you will use to store your data. We'll show you how to create tables using the wizard and build them from scratch in the Design View. Then we'll move on to fields, which we will cover in some detail: their data types, properties and validation.

Covers

Chapter Three

The Datasheet View

The Datasheet View is a window that displays data from a table in a row and column format, similar to that of Microsoft Excel. In the Datasheet View you can view, edit, add, delete, sort and search for data.

Opening a Table in the Datasheet View

1 Click on the **Open** button in the Database Window toolbar, or ...

2 Double-click on the table itself

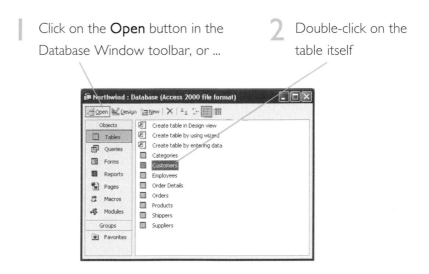

Components of the Datasheet View

Drag cursor to resize columns

Field (column)

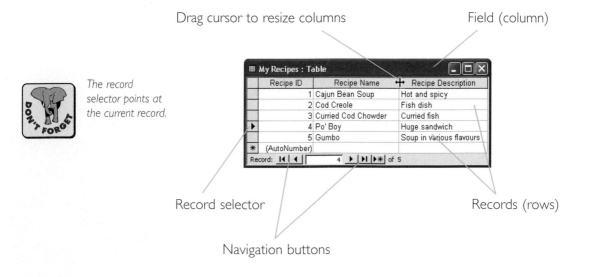

The record selector points at the current record.

Record selector

Records (rows)

Navigation buttons

Looking at Tables in the Datasheet View

Using the Navigation Buttons

Use the navigation buttons to move around the table when editing.

Use the navigation buttons to move through the data in your table:

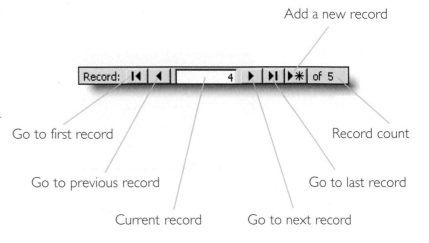

Add a new record

Go to first record

Record count

Take care when looking at records. Any changes you make will be saved when you move to another record.

Go to previous record

Go to last record

Current record

Go to next record

Sorting Table Data

1 Click on the field name to sort by

Access displays the fields in the same order as they appear in the table design. To change the order they appear in the datasheet, change the order in the design.

2 Click on the Ascending (A-Z) or Descending (Z-A) buttons on the toolbar

Freezing Columns in the Table

Sometimes, especially when a table has a lot of fields, it is helpful to "freeze" one column as a reference while you look at the others. Freezing a column locks that field in the left-most position no matter where you scroll horizontally in the rest of the table.

To unlock the column, select the Format Menu > Unfreeze All Columns option.

1 Click on the field name to highlight that column

2 Select the **Format menu > Freeze Columns** option

Adding Records in the Datasheet View

With the table open in the Datasheet View, you are ready to begin entering new records.

1 Click on the **New** button on the navigation bar

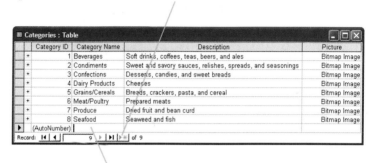

2 Type the record data in the empty fields

Moving and Copying Data

In common with all Office 2003 applications, Access makes it easy to move or copy items (otherwise known as "cutting and pasting", or "copy and pasting"), saving you time when entering lots of repetitive data.

For speed, you can use the keyboard shortcuts: CTRL+X to cut, CTRL+C to copy and CTRL+P to paste.

Cut   Copy   Paste

1 Highlight the item you wish to copy using the mouse

If you have the Office Clipboard active, you can cut/copy and paste multiple items. Use the Options drop-down at the bottom of the Task Pane to activate and deactivate the Clipboard.

2 Click the **Cut** (to move) or **Copy** (to copy!) button on the toolbar

3 The selected item appears in the Clipboard task pane

4 Click on the place where you wish to place the selection and then on the **Paste** button

Making Changes in the Datasheet View

Editing Record Data

Use the navigation buttons, the **Edit > Go To** menu option or simply click to select the record you want to change.

Any changes you make to a record are saved when you move to another record, although you can use the Edit > Undo menu option to correct typing errors.

| To change the data that's in the field, just click in the field box and type your changes

⊞ Categories : Table				
	Category ID	Category Name	Description	Picture
+	1	Beverages	Soft drinks, coffees, teas, beers, and ales	Bitmap Image
+	2	Condiments	Sweet and savory sauces, relishes, spreads, and seasonings	Bitmap Image
+	3	Confections	Desserts, candies, and sweet breads	Bitmap Image
+	4	Dairy Products	Cheeses	Bitmap Image
+	5	Grains/Cereals	Breads, crackers, pasta, and cereal	Bitmap Image
+	6	Meat/Poultry	Prepared meats	Bitmap Image
+	7	Produce	Dried fruit and bean curd	Bitmap Image
+	8	Seafood	Seaweed and fish	Bitmap Image
*	(AutoNumber)			

Record: I◄ ◄ 8 ► ►I ►* of 8

To delete a record, click on the record selector to highlight the record. Then press the DELETE key.

2 To completely replace the contents of a field, point the mouse at its left side until the cursor changes into a big plus sign. Click once with the mouse and the field will empty. Type your changes

Resizing Columns and Rows

By default, all the columns are the same width, so you might have to resize them to see their contents properly. You can resize rows too. Move the mouse between the column headings or record selectors until the cursor changes to a bar with a double-headed arrow. Drag the cursor and release when at the right size.

Double click on the field name and the column will resize automatically to fit the contents.

Moving Columns

The columns are arranged in the same order as they appear in the Design View. To change this order in the Datasheet View, click on the column heading so that the whole column is selected. Click again and hold down the left mouse button while dragging the column to the desired position. Release the mouse button to place the column.

If columns are getting in the way, you can hide them temporarily by using the Format > Hide Columns option. Bring them back with the Format > Unhide Columns option.

Finding and Replacing Data

Access will not search a subdatasheet unless the Find option is invoked while the cursor is in a subdatasheet record. In that case, it will only search the data source of the subdatasheet and not the main table.

If a table is very large it might not be practical to keep scrolling down until you find the record you want. Fortunately Access makes it easy to search for values. Select the **Edit > Find** menu option and enter the criteria for your search in the dialog box:

1 Enter the search text here

2 Choose to search either one field or the whole table

The "Search Fields as Formatted" option looks for the field based on its Format, rather than the underlying value. Refer to Access Help for information regarding Formats. Check the "Match Case" option if the search needs to be case-sensitive.

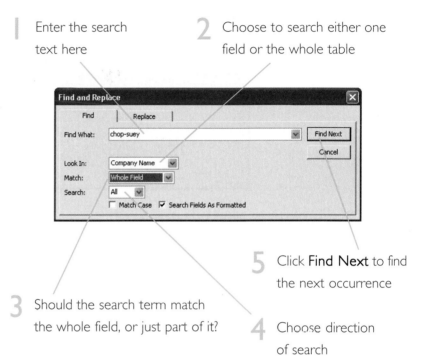

5 Click **Find Next** to find the next occurrence

3 Should the search term match the whole field, or just part of it?

4 Choose direction of search

You can search for imprecise values using "wildcards". Consult Access Help for a list of the wildcards supported.

Replacing Data

1 Click on the Replace tab and fill in the search criteria as before

2 Enter the value which will replace any instances of the search term in the "Replace With" box

3 Choose "Replace" to replace the current instance; "Find Next" to skip to the next instance; or "Replace All" to replace all occurrences without being given the opportunity to review them

Looking at Subdatasheets

A Subdatasheet contains data related to the main datasheet. It helps you view the contents of linked tables without having to keep switching between them. When a table is in a one-to-one relationship, or on the "one" side of a one-to-many relationship with another table, Access creates a subdatasheet automatically, but you can add a subdatasheet to any table (or form or query, as we shall see later on).

We'll learn more about Relationships in Chapter 4.

Looking at a Table's Subdatasheet

1 Click on the plus sign in the left-hand column of the table to expand the subdatasheet

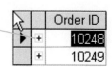

2 The subdatasheet expands to show the data in the linked table

A subdatasheet can be navigated, sorted and otherwise manipulated in exactly the same way as any other datasheet.

	Order ID	Customer	Employee	Order Date	Required Date	Shipped Date
	10248	Wilman Kala	Buchanan, Steven	Jul-04-2004	Aug-01-2004	Jul-16-2004

	Product	Unit Price	Quantity	Discount
	Queso Cabrales	$14.00	12	0%
	Singaporean Hokkien Fried Mee	$9.80	10	0%
	Mozzarella di Giovanni	$34.80	5	0%
*		$0.00	1	0%

	Order ID	Customer	Employee	Order Date	Required Date	Shipped Date
+	10249	Tradição Hipermercados	Suyama, Michael	Jul-05-2004	Aug-16-2004	Jul-10-2004
+	10250	Hanari Carnes	Peacock, Margaret	Jul-08-2004	Aug-05-2004	Jul-12-2004
+	10251	Victuailles en stock	Leverling, Janet	Jul-08-2004	Aug-05-2004	Jul-15-2004

3 Click on the minus sign to collapse the subdatasheet

Subdatasheets can be nested up to eight levels deep, but each datasheet or subdatasheet can have only one nested subdatasheet. For example, the Northwind database Customers table can contain one Orders table subdatasheet, and the Orders table subdatasheet can contain one Order Details subdatasheet. But the Customers table can't contain both an Orders table subdatasheet and a Salespeople query subdatasheet.

Creating a Table with the Table Wizard

Like the Database Wizard, the Table Wizard can help you create a table quickly using various templates as a starting point. You can always go back and "fine tune" it afterwards.

Double-click "Create table by using wizard" in the Tables pane of the Database Window

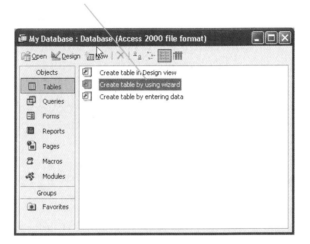

Choose from either Personal or Business templates

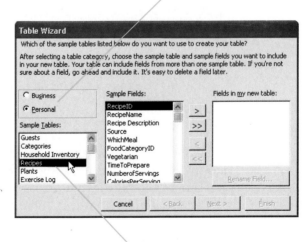

Select a template

4 Click on the field(s) you require

Use the "Rename Field" option to give your field a more descriptive name if you think it needs one. Field names can be up to 64 characters long, so use them to their best advantage!

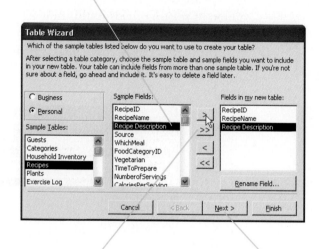

5 Use the selection buttons to include the fields you want

6 Click **Next**

7 Give the table a name

All tables should have a Primary Key so that every record is unique (see p. 48)

(see p. 48)

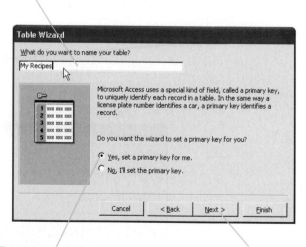

Access can generate a Primary Key for you called an Autonumber (see p.48). This is generally a good idea, unless the key needs to describe the record – e.g. you might want to list machine parts using a descriptive Part Number field.

(see p.48)

8 Let Access set a Primary Key

9 Click **Next**

The steps in this section will only appear if you already have tables in your database.

Setting Table Relationships

If there are other tables in your database, Access gives you the option of relating fields in this new table to those in an existing table. Otherwise the wizard proceeds directly to the stage described in "Completing the Wizard and Creating the Table" on p. 41.

The relationships you define between the tables are what gives Access its power and flexibility. See the discussion on Relational Databases in Chapter 1.

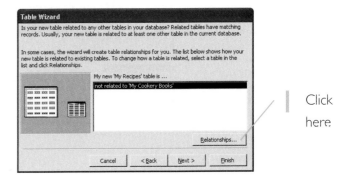

Click here

Let's assume in this example that our new "My Recipes" table is going to be related to the "My Cookery Books" table. Because one cookery book will contain many recipes, we're going to establish a many-to-one relationship between the "My Recipes" and "My Cookery Books" tables. We'll look at table relationships in greater detail in the next chapter.

2 Specify the relationship

3 Click **OK**

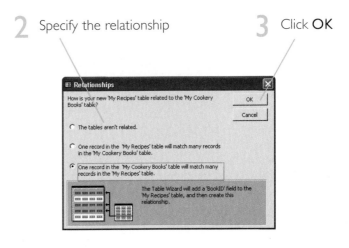

4 Access updates the list of relationships for the table

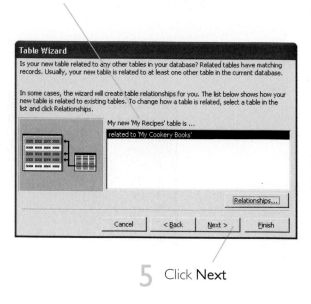

5 Click **Next**

The wizard jumps straight to this stage if there are no other tables in your database.

Completing the Wizard and Creating the Table

If once the table has been created you wish to start entering data into the datasheet straight away, select the "Enter data directly into the table" option.

10 Specify "Enter data ..."

11 Click **Finish**

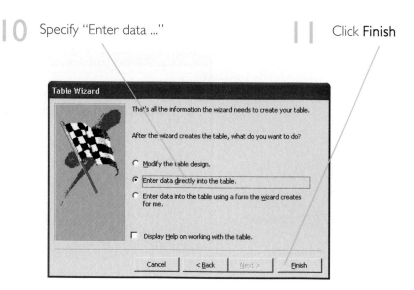

Creating a Table in the Design View

Here we will look at the process for creating a table from scratch in the Design view.

1 Double Click on "Create table in Design view"

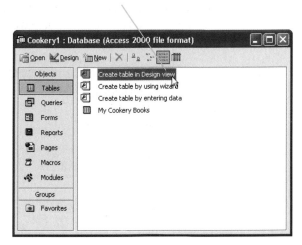

2 The empty Table Design View appears:

Lower pane is for setting field properties

Upper pane is for specifying field information

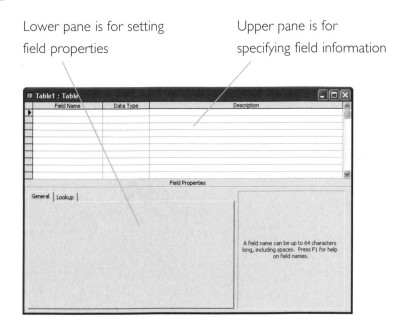

The text in the right-hand panel of the lower pane changes when you move from area to area and provides useful information.

Adding a Field to a Table

The Table Design View

In the upper pane you enter field definition information, such as the name of the field, the type of data it will store, and (optionally) a description. You also specify the primary key here.

In the lower pane you can set field properties which control how the data in the field will be displayed; what constitutes valid data for the field; the size of the data it will store and many other attributes.

Right click on the field selector to insert or delete fields. You can use cut and paste to change the order of fields.

Adding a Field to the Table

Use the TAB key to move between the rows and columns in the Table Design View and enter the field attributes as shown below.

Repeat steps 1-4 to add extra fields.

To delete a field, select it and press the DELETE key. Take care if the field forms part of a query, form or report as it may cause it to stop working.

Access will not let you delete a field that is a link in a relationship to another table without deleting the relationship first.

1 Enter the field name(s) here

2 Select the field's data type from the list

Field Selector

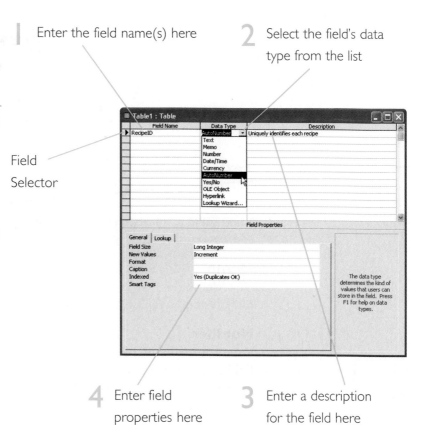

4 Enter field properties here

3 Enter a description for the field here

Choosing Field Data Types

All these data types are explained in great detail in Access Help.

When considering which data types to use for a field you need to consider:

- What kind of values will be stored in the field?

- How will you use the data stored in the field?

For instance, if you want a part number that includes letters as well as numbers, you will need a Text field. If you want to add field values together, you must remember that this is only possible with Number and Currency fields.

You have already seen the list of data types available in Access, when you learned how to add a new field to your table in the last section. Now we're going to look at each in turn.

List of data types in the Table Design View

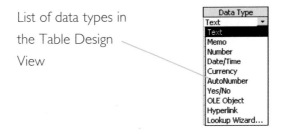

Text
This is the most commonly used of all the data types. It can contain up to 255 alphanumeric characters, with the default length being set at 50 characters. You would use this type for name, address or other descriptive fields.

Memo
The Memo field is for longer text entries, such as general notes. It can store up to 65,535 characters.

Number
You should use the Number data type when you intend to use the field as a basis for calculations, e.g. an Hourly Rate field for a job, which you would multiply by the Hours Worked field (another Number field) to calculate a fee, or where you might need to sort based on the field's value – e.g. to rank salespeople based on their results, you would make the Results field a Number.

Currency

The Currency data type is a special sort of numerical field which is specifically for monetary values. It can be used in calculations like a Number field.

Autonumber

Use the Autonumber data type to ensure that each record in the Table has a unique value in this field, which is assigned automatically by Access when a new record is created. It is therefore ideal for primary key fields (see p. 48)

Date/Time

If you use this data type to store all your date and time information, Access lets you sort the values chronologically, display dates in different formats and calculate elapsed time.

Yes/No

Sometimes called the "Boolean" field, the Yes/No data type includes just two possible values: Yes and No. In the Datasheet View it appears as a checkbox – empty for "No" and checked for "Yes".

This data type is ideal for true/false, completed/not completed, include/don't include and similar information.

OLE Object

This data type is used when you want to link or embed an object external to Access, such as a Word document, graphic or sound file.

Hyperlink

This is a special type of field for storing links to other locations, such as web URLs (Uniform Resource Locators).

Lookup

A Lookup field restricts data entry to a limited set of values that you specify in the Lookup Wizard. These can be static values, or derived from another table. If you have a Widgets table for instance, you might create a Color lookup field and limit the choice to "blue", "red" or "white".

Setting Field Properties

Just about everything in Access has a number of properties you can use to alter its appearance or behavior and fields are no exception. Some field properties you will never need to change. Others, like Field Size, you might adjust for every field you create.

Some properties are common across all fields, others are specific to certain types. For instance, Number and Currency fields have a Decimal Places property, while other types do not.

In this section we are going to list some of the more common field properties. To find out what a particular property does, refer to the Field Properties pane at the bottom of the Table Design View. The names and values of the properties are listed on the left and the area to the right displays information about that property. Press the F1 key to bring up the relevant pages in Access Help.

Click on the field property to change it

You can press F1 to display information about the current property.

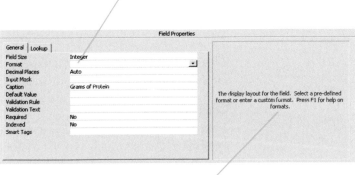

2 Access displays helpful information about the property

Field Size

For most databases Long Integer (for whole numbers) and Doubles (for real numbers) will be sufficient.

For a text field, Field Size specifies the maximum of number of characters that can be stored. The maximum is 255 characters and the default size is 50 characters. For Number and Currency fields, things are more complicated. Although the default value is Long Integer, there are several other possible sizes: Byte, Integer, Long Integer, Single, Double, Replication ID and Decimal.

For a detailed explanation of Formats and Input Masks, refer to Access Help.

Format

Specifies how the field will be displayed.

Input Mask

Allows you to create a format or pattern in which data must be entered. For example, you can insist that telephone numbers include international codes.

Decimal Places

The number of decimal places for Number and Currency fields.

Caption

A descriptive name for the field, as it will appear on forms. By default, Access uses the field name.

Default Value

Here you can specify a value for the field when the record is created.

Validation Rule

An expression that limits the range of allowable values in the field. For example, you won't want numbers in a Surname field.

Validation Text

The message displayed to the user when the Validation Rule is not adhered to.

Required

If an entry in the field is mandatory, you should set its Required property to "Yes". The default is "No".

Allow Zero Length

This property specifies whether empty text strings can be entered. It is useful when a field must contain data, but you don't know yet what the value is.

You can save time by using smart tags to perform actions in Microsoft Office Access 2003 that you'd usually have to open other programs for. In Access, you can attach smart tags to a table or query or to controls on a form, report, or data access page.

Index

A field can be marked as an index field to speed up searches and sorts performed on it. The default value is "No".

Smart Tags

Specifies which Smart Tags are applied to the field.

Choosing a Primary Key

The Primary Key of a table is a field that uniquely identifies each record within it. Access uses the primary key in sorting and indexing operations. The easiest way of ensuring that a primary key field is unique is to make it an Autonumber field.

Any field which contains unique values can be used as a Primary Key. Autonumbering the records just makes it the responsibility of Access to keep those values unique.

Follow the steps below to make an Autonumber field the primary key:

1 Select the Autonumber field type in the Table Design View

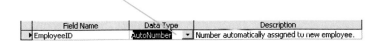

*To remove the primary key, just select the field that is currently the primary key and click the **Primary Key** button again.*

2 While the field is selected, click the **Primary Key** button on the Toolbar

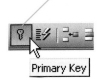

Primary Key

3 The field is marked with the Primary Key symbol in the Table Design View

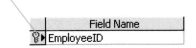

Setting a Multiple-Field Primary Key

If one field alone won't make a record unique in the table, you can specify a multiple-field primary key. Simply hold down the CTRL key while you select the fields which make up your key and then click on the Primary Key button on the Toolbar as before.

Access marks all the fields you have chosen as primary keys.

Creating Indexes

Indexing a table makes it faster for Access to find and sort its records. An index contains a "pointer" to the location of the data, rather than the actual data itself, in a similar way that this book's index directs you to the relevant page.

If a field has lots of records with the same value, indexing it won't help very much.

The primary key is indexed automatically. Other fields are likely candidates for indexing if you will be searching for or sorting on them frequently to improve performance, or if you intend to use that field as a link in a relationship with another table.

Creating an Index

1 With the table open in Design view, click the **Indexes** button on the toolbar

You can specify up to ten fields in one index, with a mixture of ascending and descending orders for the fields.

2 Click in an empty field and type a name for the index

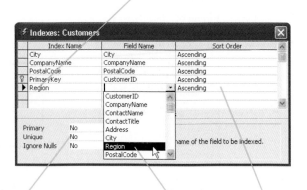

5 Allow duplicates?

4 Specify the sort order

3 Choose the Index field from the drop-down list

As with all changes to tables and other database objects, remember to save them!

Inserting a Subdatasheet into a Table

To insert a Subdatasheet into a table, first open the table in the Datasheet View.

Then, select the "Subdatasheet..." option from the **Insert** menu:

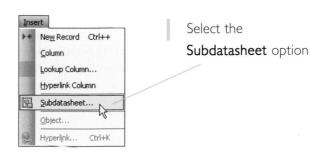

Select the **Subdatasheet** option

2 If the Subdatasheet data is coming from another table, select the Tables tab

6 Click **OK**

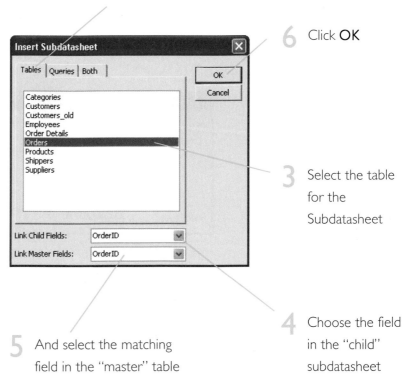

3 Select the table for the Subdatasheet

4 Choose the field in the "child" subdatasheet

5 And select the matching field in the "master" table

To remove a Subdatasheet, select the **Format** *>* **Subdatasheet** *>* **Remove** *menu option.*

Validating Data at Field Level

Access can help you ensure that only valid data makes it into your table by letting you specify certain rules which any data you input must obey. By using field validation, you can limit the data to a specific value or range of values which Access checks when you move away from the current field. You can then display your own custom message to display to the user if the data is not valid.

In this example, we're going to ensure that any new Orders in the Orders Table have an OrderDate of today's date or later. Open the Orders Table in the Design view and proceed as follows:

Select the OrderDate field

"Date()" is one of many functions in Access. This one returns the current date. We use the "greater than" sign followed by the equals sign to test for a date that is today's or later.

2 Type ">=Date()" in the Validation Rule box

3 Type the message to display in the Validation Text box

4 When the user enters a date in this field earlier than today's, our error message is displayed

Validating Data at Record Level

When validation takes place at record level, the whole record is considered before Access decides whether it can be saved or not. As such it is useful when the validation of one field depends on the value of another field within that record – which is impossible to test at the field level.

The process for setting up validation rules at record level is very similar to field level validation, except the rule is defined at the table, rather than field level.

In some situations Access requires the field names to be enclosed by square brackets.
This is one of them.

1   Type in the Validation Rule – here, the Shipping Date must be later than the Order Date

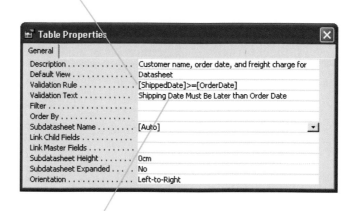

2   Type in the message to display if the rule is not followed

3   When the Shipping Date is earlier than the Order Date Access shows an error message:

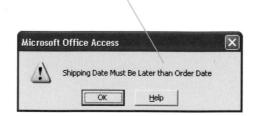

Relationships

We've already seen how important it is to create relationships between your tables. In this chapter we're going to be looking at the mechanics of doing this. First we're going to talk about the different ways in which tables can be related and then we're going to show you how to create those relationships using Access. We'll teach you how to work with the relationships in the Relationship Window and discuss Referential Integrity, which is a big term for a simple, but vital, topic.

Covers

Chapter Four

Introduction to Table Relationships

We've already seen how important it is to create relationships between tables. As well as helping us to make more sense of our data, it also avoids duplication of data which is inefficient and can result in errors.

There are three different types of relationship: one-to-many, one-to-one and many-to-many.

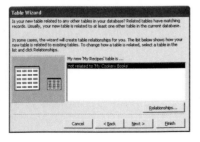

You can create relationships at any time, but it's best to do it when you first create the tables. You can also create temporary relationships in a query, but it's often better to create a permanent relationship like we're showing you here.

One-to-Many

This is the most widely-used relationship. One table (the "parent") can have many matching records in another table (the "child"). For example, one Supplier table record could have many matching Product records, because one supplier will typically stock several products. The field in the parent table is called the Primary Key and must be unique (see p. 48). The field in the child table is called the Foreign Key and does not have to be unique, although data retrieval can be faster if the Foreign Key is indexed (see p. 49).

One-to-One

A record in one table matches one record in another. Both are linked by their primary keys. You might want to do this for security, e.g. splitting credit card numbers across two tables, but it is not commonly used.

Many-to-Many

A record in one table can have many matching records in another and vice versa. To achieve this in Access, you need to create a "Junction Table" and then relate the two tables to this junction table using *two* one-to-many relationships. The Northwind Orders and Products table are related in this way, using the Order Details table as a junction table.

Table wizard

In the last chapter, we saw how the Table Wizard can help us define relationships. But to harness the full power of Access, we're going to have to learn how to create those relationships ourselves. We do this in the Table Relationships Window and we'll be looking at that next.

The Table Relationships Window

Before you can create relationships between tables, you have to add the tables to the Table Relationships window.

1 To open the Table Relationships window, select the **Tools > Relationships** menu option, or click the **Relationships** button on the Database toolbar

2 If no relationships have been defined, the Show Table dialog box appears and the Relationships Window is blank; otherwise you can bring up the Show Table dialog box using the **Show Table** toolbar button

To select a block of tables, click on the first table, then hold down the SHIFT key while clicking on the last table in the block. To select multiple tables that aren't adjacent, hold down the CTRL key while clicking on the tables.

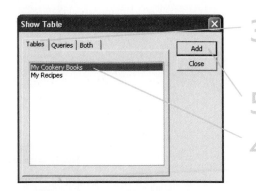

3 Select a tab to see tables, queries or both

5 Click **Add**

4 Click on the table you want to see

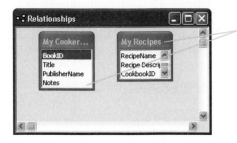

6 The tables appear in the window, ready for you to define the relationships between them

It's often a good idea to include all the tables in the window, whether you want to create relationships between them or not. The relationships window then shows "at a glance" the structure of your database.

7 Repeat steps 1-5 until you have all the tables you want to see in the relationships window

Relating Two Tables

Drawing the Relationship Line

To create a relationship between two tables, simply drag a field from one table to another field on the other table.

Both source and destination field should be of the same data type (see p. 44), unless the Primary Key is an Autonumber field. You can match an Autonumber field with a Number field if the FieldSize property of both fields is the same.

1 Click on the primary key (bold) and hold the mouse button down

2 Drag the primary key to the foreign key of the second table and release

3 The Edit Relationships window appears

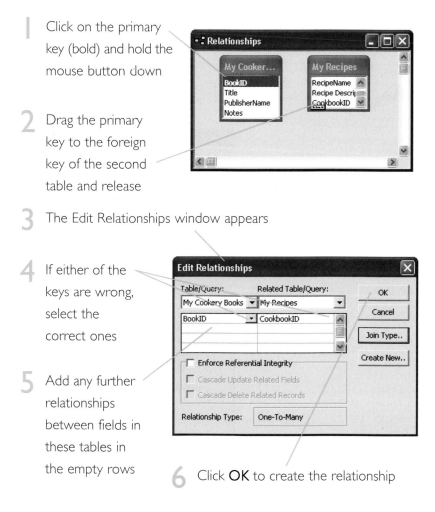

4 If either of the keys are wrong, select the correct ones

5 Add any further relationships between fields in these tables in the empty rows

6 Click **OK** to create the relationship

Access represents this relationship as a line drawn between the two tables in the Relationships Window.

Note that Access works out automatically what type of relationship this is. Here it assumes one-to-many because one of the fields is a primary key and the other is not. If both fields were primary keys Access would assume a one-to-one relationship. If *neither* field is a primary key, Access won't make any guesses and will call it "indeterminate" instead.

Specifying the Join Type

The join type is not the same as the relationship type. The join type lets you specify which records will appear in any queries that use the related tables when records appear in one table and not the other(s). For example, if one of our cookbooks doesn't yet contain any recipes, we might decide to leave that cookbook out of any query results. The join type does not affect the underlying relationship in any way.

Right click on the line representing the relationship and on the pop-up menu select **Edit Relationship**

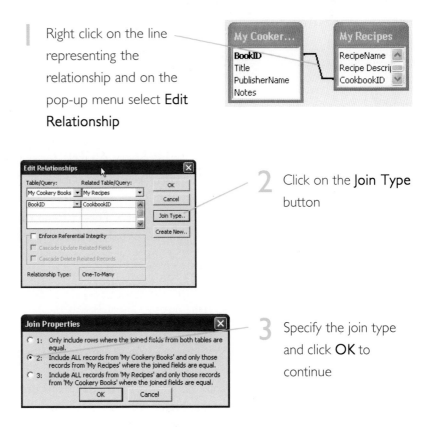

Click on the **Join Type** button

Specify the join type and click **OK** to continue

4 The relationship line changes to an arrow pointing at the "CookbookID" field

You can move the tables around in the window and the relationship lines will be adjusted automatically. Once you have a layout you like, save it.

A line without an arrow on the relationship diagram is called an *inner join*. A line with an arrow is called an *outer join*. In the case of an outer join, the arrow points at the field where the values must match to be included in the query results.

Saving the Relationship Details

Any new relationships you create, or existing ones you change will be saved automatically. If you change the layout of the diagram then you will be asked if you want to save the new layout when you close it.

Viewing Relationships

Removing a table from the layout does not delete the relationship. To delete the relationship, click on the line between the tables and press the DELETE key.

You can choose which relationships are shown in the Relationship Window. Use the **Tools > Relationships** menu option, or the toolbar buttons as shown below:

Click the **Show All Relationships** button to see all the relationships in your database

Click the **Show Direct Relationships** to see only the relationships for the table currently highlighted in the Database Window

Clear the layout (does not delete the relationships)

You can print the relationships diagram for use as documentation. Choose the File > Print Relationships menu option.

To hide a table, use the **Relationships > Hide** menu option. When you next open the window that table will reappear, unless you save the layout. To restore all the tables to the layout, click the **Show All Relationships** toolbar button or choose the **Relationships > Show All Relationships** menu option.

Enforcing Referential Integrity

When you enforce referential integrity, you are asking Access to keep an eye on any records that might be "orphaned" when you delete records from a table which is in a relationship. Access tidies up all the loose ends depending on rules you specify. You set these rules in the Edit Relationships window:

1 Check this box to switch on referential integrity

2 Use these options to specify rules for updated records

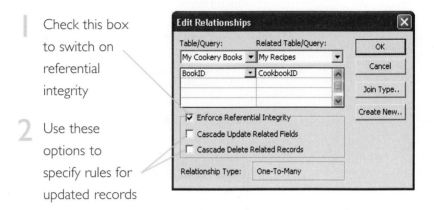

When referential integrity is enforced, if you try to delete a record from the parent table; change a primary key in a record which has related records; or change a key in the child table to a value that does not exist in the parent table, then Access won't let you.

Cascading Updates and Deletions

You can however request that Access deals with any such changes or deletions automatically, by checking one or both "Cascade" options. With the Cascade Deletions rule turned on, if a parent record is deleted then Access will automatically delete all related child records. With Cascade Updates turned on, you can change the value of a primary key in the parent table and Access will automatically update the child records.

Any relationships which include referential integrity are depicted differently in the relationships diagram, with a "1" symbol on the "one" side and an infinity symbol on the "many" side of the relationship.

Creating a Many-to-Many Relationship

In a many-to-many relationship, a record in one table can have many matching records in another table. In such a relationship, neither table is the parent. To create this type of relationship we need to have an intermediary table, known as a Junction Table.

The junction table contains new fields which have the same characteristics as the primary key fields from each of the other two tables. Within the junction table, these fields are set to be primary keys, but will act as foreign keys to the two tables we want to relate.

For example: the Northwind database uses the Order Details table as the junction table for the many-to-many relationship between Orders and Products. It has two primary keys – ProductID and OrderID, one from each of Products and Orders.

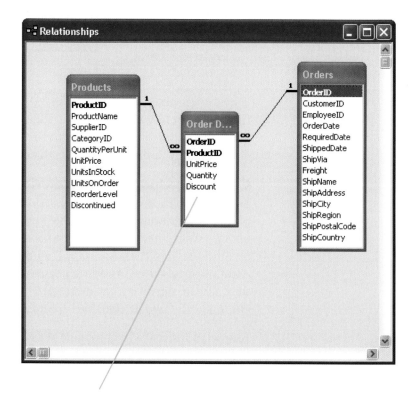

The Order Details table acts as the Junction Table between the Products and Orders Table

Importing and Exporting Data

One of this product's great strengths is its ability to interface with other applications. If you have information stored in another format, such as in a text file or an Excel spreadsheet, then Access has the tools to import that data into a table. Access can also export table data into formats suitable for other applications. In this chapter we'll be looking at how this is done and also how Access can "link" to tables held in other databases.

Covers

Chapter Five

Importing Access Database Objects

You can import database objects from other Access databases. This is especially useful if you have already created an object in one database that you could adapt for use in another.

When you import objects from other databases, what you end up with is a copy of that object. Any changes you make will not be reflected in the original and vice-versa.

Select the **File > Get External Data > Import** menu option.

2 From the Import dialog box, select the database which contains the objects you want to import. Make sure the "Files of Type" box specifies Microsoft Access

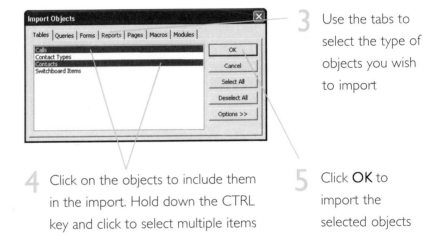

3 Use the tabs to select the type of objects you wish to import

4 Click on the objects to include them in the import. Hold down the CTRL key and click to select multiple items

5 Click **OK** to import the selected objects

The objects you imported will now be available in the Database Window.

Import Options
Click on the **Options** button to see the other import options you can specify:

If you just want the table structure and not its data, select "Definition Only" in the Import Options.

Importing Data from Excel

Before you import data from an Excel spreadsheet, make sure that the spreadsheet data is in a tabular format – i.e. each record corresponds to a row in the spreadsheet – and all the columns are lined up properly.

You will normally create a new table to store this data, but if the Excel datasheet column headings correspond exactly to the field names in an existing table, you can use the Import Wizard to append the spreadsheet data to that table.

1   Select the **File > Get External Data > Import** menu option

2   From the Import dialog box, select the spreadsheet which contains the data you want to import. Make sure the "Files of Type" box specifies the correct version of Microsoft Excel

3   The Import Wizard starts. If your Excel spreadsheet contains more than one worksheet or named range, choose which to include

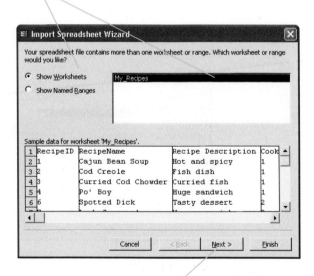

4   Click **Next** to move to page two of the Import Wizard

5 If the first row of the spreadsheet data shown contains column headings, click the checkbox. Otherwise leave it clear

If you tell Access that the first row contains column headings but it can't use those headings as field names, you'll get an error message and Access will automatically assign new names.

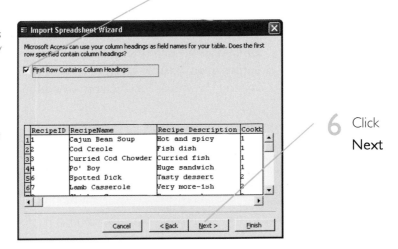

6 Click **Next**

7 Choose whether to import this data into a new table (in which case you'll have to specify a name), or into an existing one

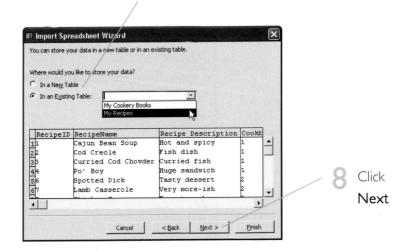

8 Click **Next**

9 If you choose to create a new table, Access displays a set of wizard pages to help you configure it (steps 10-15), otherwise it jumps to the final step (step 16)

10 Each column will become a field in the new table. Click on the columns to move from field to field

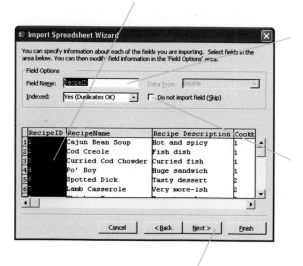

11 Accept the field name, or enter a new one

12 Check the box to skip unwanted fields

13 Repeat steps 10-13 for each column in the spreadsheet. When you're done, click Next

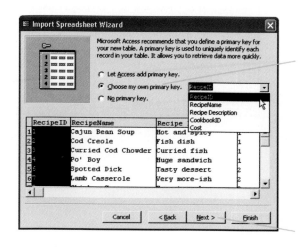

14 Select a field to be the primary key, or let Access create one for you

15 Click **Next**

16 Click **Finish** on the final page of the wizard and Access imports the data

Importing Data from Text Files

Text files are either *delimited*, where records can be different lengths and special characters are used as "markers" to show where one field ends and another begins; or *fixed width*, which means all the records are rows of data of the same length. Access can import both types, but the process for each is slightly different.

Start by selecting Text in the "Files of type" box in the Import dialog.

Importing Delimited Text Files

1 Select the text file you want to import and click **Import**

2 Specify "Delimited" in the first page of the wizard

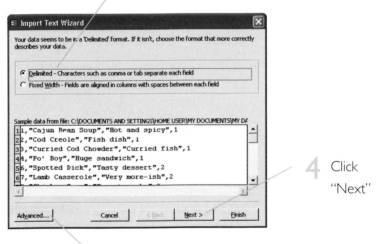

4 Click "Next"

Clicking on "Advanced" allows you to create an "Import Specification" which you can save to use with other import operations. Here you can specify which fields to import, how Access should handle date values and other criteria.

3 Click **Advanced** for further options if you need them

5 Specify which character separates the fields

6 ... and which characters surround strings of text ("" by default)

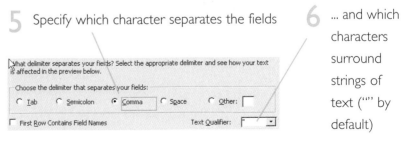

7 Click **Next** to continue

8 Choose whether to import this data into a new table (in which case you'll have to specify a name), or into an existing one

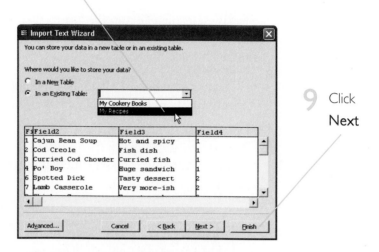

9 Click **Next**

If you are importing your data into a new table Access needs you tell it how to set it up. These steps are the same, regardless of what type of text data you are importing.

10 If you have elected to create a new table, follow Steps 10-15 on p. 65 then return here when you are done

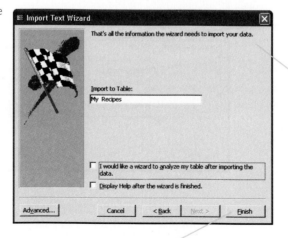

11 The wizard asks you to confirm the choices you have made

12 Click **Finish** to import the data

Importing Fixed Width Text Files

The Import Wizard behaves slightly differently when importing fixed width text files. On the second page of the wizard, you'll see an extract of your data with vertical lines between the fields and a ruler above them which marks the position of the characters in the file.

Access has made some guesses about where one field stops and another begins. If Access hasn't got it completely right, you can:

- Create a new line by clicking at the position that marks the boundary between the fields

- Delete a line by double-clicking it

- Move a line by depressing the left mouse button and dragging it to the desired position

*Click **Advanced** to create an Import Specification for your Fixed Width text files.*

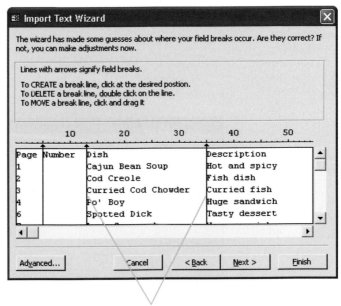

Field separation lines

In all other respects you should follow the same steps as you would to import a delimited text file.

Exporting to Other Access Databases

You can also copy objects to other databases by using copy and paste.

You can use the Access Export menu option to copy tables (and other database objects) from one Access database to another. This can be useful if you want to base a new object on an existing one.

I Highlight the object to export in the Database Window and choose the **File > Export** menu option, or right-click on it and select **Export** from the shortcut menu

2 Locate the database you want to export to in the "Export Table To" dialog box

You can export data to other formats too, just by changing the value of the "Files of Type" drop-down in the "Export Table To" dialog box. For text files you'll have to give Access more information, just as you did when importing text. We covered this on p. 66-68.

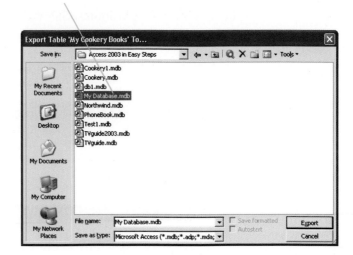

3 Choose a different name for the table in the destination database if you wish. Specify whether you want to retain just the structure of the table or the data too

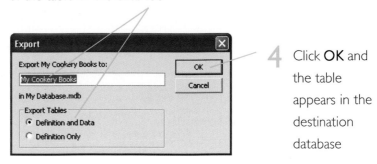

4 Click **OK** and the table appears in the destination database

Linking to Other Data Sources

As well as importing data from other sources, Access allows you to "link" to those sources. When you link to a data source any changes you make to the data in Access is reflected in the linked data and vice versa.

Generally speaking, if you know that you're only ever likely to use the data in your Access database, you should import it. There are significant performance benefits to be gained from doing so.

But you might wish to link to a table if, for example, it is part of a database that is shared over a network. By linking you can be sure that your own database has the latest version of that table's data at all times. You should also consider linking if a table is ever likely to be updated by applications other than Access.

1   Select the **File > Get External Data > Link Tables** menu option

2   Navigate to the data source you want to link to in the "Link" dialog box

3   Select the table from the list

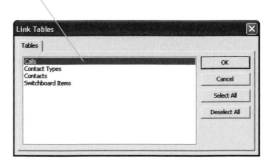

Linked tables appear with an arrow symbol in the Database Window.

4   The linked table appears in the Database Window

Forms

Access forms, like their paper counterparts, collect and organize information. Forms are the "user interface" of an Access database, providing a way to enter data and display it for review. Forms make it easier to read data on the screen and simplify movement around your application. In this chapter we'll be looking at how to create forms and use them to enter, find and present data.

Covers

Chapter Six

Creating a Form Using the Wizard

1   In the Forms tab of the Database Window, click on the **New** button ...

Give some thought to what data you want to display before you create the form. It will save you time in the long run.

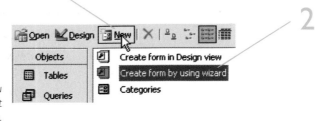

2   ... or double click on the "Create form by using wizard" link

3   The Form Wizard appears

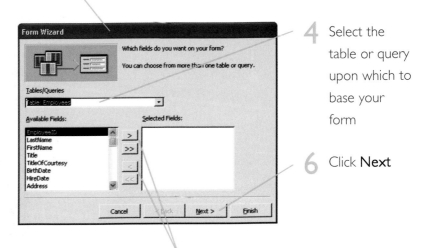

4   Select the table or query upon which to base your form

6   Click **Next**

5   Use the buttons to select fields in the table or query that you want to include on your form

7   On the next page of the wizard, select a layout for your form

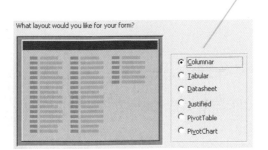

8   Click **Next**

9 Select a style for the form

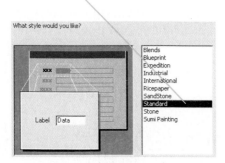

10 Give your new form a name

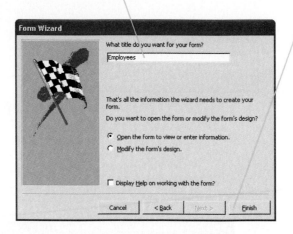

11 Click **Finish** to exit the wizard

12 Access creates the new form and fills it with data

Saving a Form

As with everything else you create using Access, you must remember to save your forms. Access will prompt you if you attempt to close a form without saving it first, but it is important to get into the habit of saving your work regularly.

For every menu option there is usually an equivalent button on the toolbar.

1 Open the File menu and click **Save**

2 If the form is a new one, Access will ask you to enter a name for it. Type it in and click **OK**

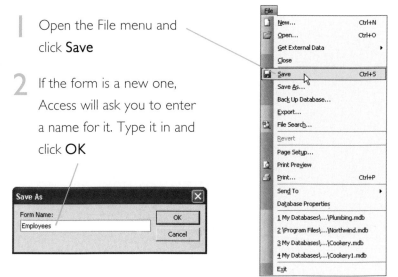

3 Access saves the form and you can now see it in the forms tab of the Database Window

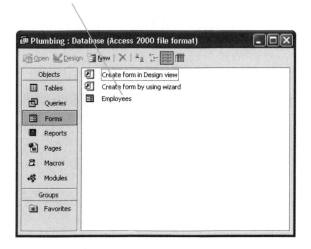

Opening a Form

To open a specific form, first make sure you are working with the database that form belongs to. Then:

1 Click the **Forms** option in the Objects bar

2 Double click on the form you want to use

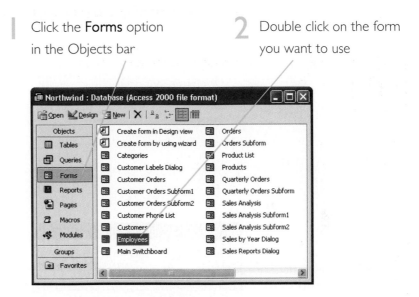

3 Access opens the form you requested

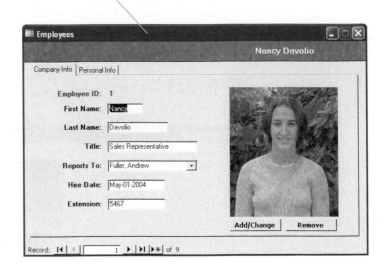

Creating a Form Using Autoforms

Access offers an even quicker way to create forms than the wizard: Autoforms. They tend to be a bit "rough and ready" and will normally require tweaking afterwards, but they're a great way to get something working quickly when you're stuck for time.

1   Highlight the table or query upon which to base the form in the Database Window

2   Click the Database Window's **New** button

3   Select the style of Autoform you want to create

Forms can get their data from queries and tables. Some forms, such as switchboard forms, don't need to be bound to a data source.

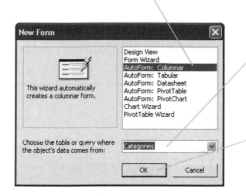

3   Select the data source from the drop-down list

4   Click **OK**

5   Access creates your form

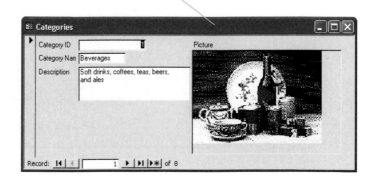

Using a Form to Add a New Record

Forms make data entry easier and more intuitive than typing data directly into tables. Like any sort of form, you start with blanks and fill in the details.

1 First, open the form you want to use (see p. 75)

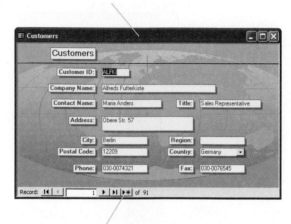

2 Click on the form's **New Record** button

To move backwards between the fields, hold down the SHIFT key while pressing TAB.

3 A blank form appears – type in the record details, using the TAB key to move from field to field

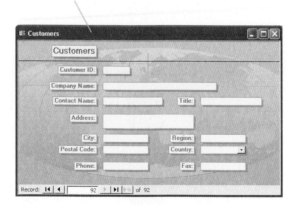

4 When you press TAB after completing the final field, Access saves the record and waits for any further data entry

Using a Form to View Data

To move between records in a form you use the navigation buttons, in the same way as you do in a datasheet (see p. 33). In this example we'll use the Northwind database Employees form.

1 The form opens to show the first record in the table

2 Click the **Next** button to move to the next record

3 Click the **Last** button to move to the final record

4 Click the **Previous** button to move back a record

5 Click the **First** button to move back to the first record

Using a Form to Edit Data

You can also use a form to modify a record within your table. As soon as you move to another record, Access saves the changes you made to the underlying table. Take care that you don't make changes inadvertently!

It's easy to make changes without meaning to, so take care when navigating your tables!

1 First, use the navigation buttons as on the previous page, to find the record you want to modify

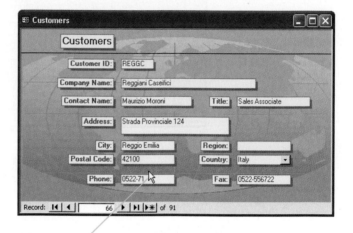

2 Click within the field you want to change and type your changes – you can either delete the existing information and start again, or just edit what is already there

3 As soon as you move to another record or close the form, the changes are saved to the table

4 You can check that your changes have been saved by moving away from the current record and then back again

Using a Form to Delete a Record

You can delete a record using a form using the "Delete Record" menu option or the **Delete** toolbar button.

1 First locate the record you want to delete

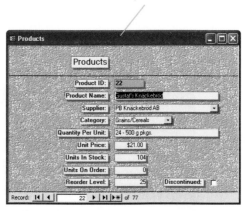

2 Choose the **Edit > Delete Record** menu option ...

3 ... or the **Delete Record** Toolbar button

*Access will only ask you to confirm deletions if you've set it up to do so. It really is a good idea because once deleted, a record is gone for good. Go to the **Tools > Options** menu item. On the "Edit/Find" tab, put a check in the Confirm panel's "Record changes" check box.*

4 Access asks you to confirm the deletion – click **Yes** to proceed

Using a Form to Find a Record

You can use a form to help you locate a specific record, just as you did with the datasheet.

1 Click on the field you want to search (here we are searching on Product Name in the Northwind Products form)

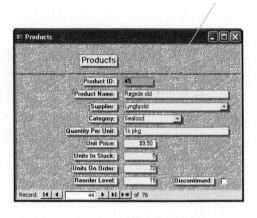

You can also use CTRL + F as a keyboard shortcut to the Find and Replace dialog box.

2 Select the **Edit > Find** menu option, or click the **Find** button on the toolbar

3 The Find and Replace dialog button opens – type the search text in the "Find What" box

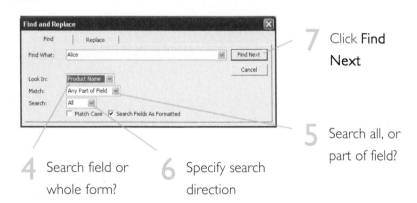

7 Click **Find Next**

5 Search all, or part of field?

4 Search field or whole form?

6 Specify search direction

Filtering Data By Selection

Filtering data allows you to restrict the records you see based on criteria that you specify. Here we are going to use the Northwind Products form and filter the records so we only see dairy products.

1   Select a record of a type that will be included in your filtered list – in this instance, a dairy product

You can filter by more than one field to narrow your selection even further.

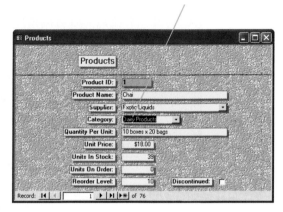

You can also display all records that do not contain a specific entry. This is called "filtering by exclusion" and is available from the **Records > Filter > Filter Excluding Selection** menu option.

2   Click on the **Filter By Selection** toolbar button

3   Access restricts the list to dairy products and updates the record count in the navigation bar

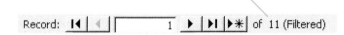

4   Move through the list of records using the navigation buttons to verify that the only products listed are dairy products

5   Click on the **Apply/Remove Filter** toolbar button to toggle the filter on and off

Filtering Data By Form

Access lets you create complex filter expressions using different operators. Consult Access help for full details.

When you filter by form, Access gives you a blank form in which to specify your filter criteria. This method allows you to enter mathematical and logical *expressions*, so it is more powerful and flexible than filtering by selection.

Here we're going to use the filter by form method to choose all seafood or dairy products that cost more than $20.

I Click the "Filter by Form" button on the toolbar

2 On the blank form provided, enter the filter criteria – in this instance, we will choose products of type "Seafood" and Unit Price ">20" (i.e. greater than $20)

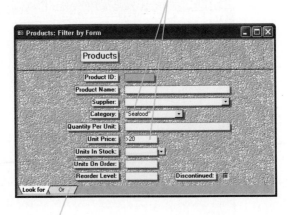

You can specify more than one "OR" clause in subsequent "OR" tabs.

3 Click on the "OR" tab and enter "Dairy Products" in the Product Category field and ">20" in the Unit Price field

4 Click on the **Apply Filter** toolbar button to filter the list of records

5 Click on the button again to toggle between filter on/off

Creating a Form in the Design View

You can create a form from scratch in the Design View. Simply click on the **New** button on the forms tab of the database window, or double click on the "Create form in Design view" link. The only difference is that if you use the "New" button, Access gives you the option of selecting a table or query upon which to base your form. Otherwise you'll have to specify it yourself in the form's *Record Source* property (see p. 89).

Components of the Form Design View

If you specify a table or query on which the form is based, you'll also see a list of fields that are in that table or query.

Form Design Toolbar   Formatting (Form/Report) Toolbar

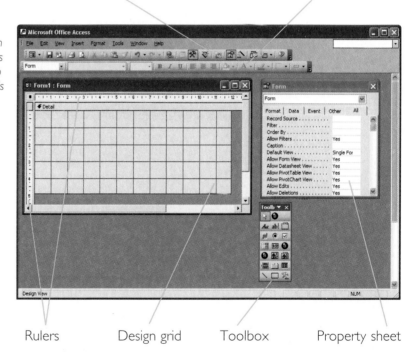

Rulers   Design grid   Toolbox   Property sheet

Remember to save the form when you have made any changes!

Within the Form Design View you have complete control over how the form looks and behaves. You add controls like text boxes, buttons, etc to the form by dragging them from the toolbox to the design grid. By setting different properties in the property sheet you can change the appearance and behavior of individual controls and the form as a whole. We'll see how to perform some of the more common tasks in the rest of this chapter.

Using Controls

A control is just a graphical object that you put on a form or report. It can be purely cosmetic like a picture, or it can be used to perform an action or display data. Putting any type of control on a form involves the same three steps:

- Click on the tool you require in the toolbox

- "Draw" the control on the form

- Set its properties in the Property sheet

There are three different types of control in Access: *Bound* controls, *Unbound* controls and *Calculated* controls.

Unbound Controls

Are not affected by the underlying data and remain static when the data changes. The label we will add to the form header on p. 86 is an example of an unbound control.

Bound Controls

A bound control derives its value from a field in the underlying table. When the data changes, so does the value of the control. In the Northwind database, those areas of the form that change as you move from record to record are bound controls.

Calculated Controls

A calculated control gets its value from an *expression*, which is a combination of mathematical or logical operations, field names, functions and so on that evaluate to a single result. For example, the value of the "Total Cost" textbox may be derived from adding the "Material Cost" field from the "Materials" table to a value the user enters in a "Cost of Labor" textbox. If the calculation depends on the underlying data (as this example does) then the control's value will be recalculated as the data changes.

Types of control include labels, text boxes, combo boxes, list boxes, command buttons, option buttons, check boxes and images. There are many other diverse controls, but the principles of placing and customizing them are very similar.

To see more controls in the toolbox, select **Add or Remove Buttons > Toolbox > More Controls** from the toolbox menu.

Adding Headers and Footers

A lot of techniques you'll learn in this and subsequent pages are used in designing reports too, so follow carefully and don't be afraid to experiment!

When you first create a form, all you see is the detail section. You can add *header* and *footer* sections to display information at the top and bottom of the form respectively, which remain static when you move from record to record in the detail section.

There are two types of header and footer. *Form* headers and footers are visible on the form. *Page* headers and footers only appear when you preview or print the form.

Headers are a good place to put a title for your form and that's what we'll do here.

You can put labels anywhere on your form using the same method we describe here. You don't have to be in the header section.

1 While in the design view, select the **View > Form Header/ Footer** menu option

2 Click the Label control in the toolbox

3 "Draw" the label onto the form header

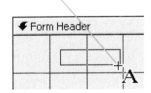

You can find the font properties in the Format tab of the Property sheet

4 Type your text into the label and hit RETURN

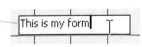

Make sure the label control "has the focus" before setting properties, otherwise you might be setting properties for another control or the form itself. A control has the focus when it is surrounded by black squares in the design view. See p. 91.

5 Change the font properties for the label

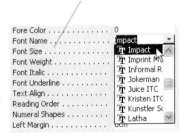

6 Choose the **View > Form** menu option to see your form in action

Adding Controls Using the Field List

A quick way to get your form displaying data from your table is to use the Field List. If you created the form by using the Database Window's **New** button you would have been given the option of specifying a table or query which your form would be based on and the Field List would have been displayed automatically:

Field List for form based on the Northwind **Customers** table

Otherwise you're going to have to specify an underlying data source for the form using it's "Control Source" property:

Specifying a Data Source for a Form

1   Click on the form to make sure it has the focus

2   If the Property sheet is not visible, click on the **Properties** toolbar button

3   In Control Source, on the Data tab of the property sheet, select the table or query upon which to base the form

4   The Field List displays the fields in your chosen table or query

We could add these controls using the toolbox. What we're demonstrating here is a quicker way to add bound controls to your form.

Adding Bound Controls

When you add a field from the field list to your form design, Access automatically creates a bound control that displays data from a field in the underlying table. It also creates a label based on the field name, which you can alter by changing the Caption property in the label's Property sheet.

1 Holding down the CTRL key, click on the fields you want on your form

2 "Drag" the fields from the field list to the design grid and release the mouse button

You can also change the label text by modifying the label's Caption property.

3 Access creates labelled controls bound to fields in your table or query

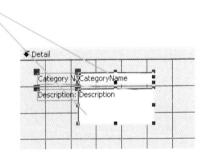

4 Run the form by choosing the **View > Form View** menu option

5 Use the navigation buttons to move between records and watch the values in the text boxes change

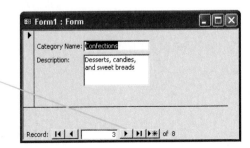

Changing Form and Control Properties

You can alter the appearance or behavior of a form or one of its constituent controls by changing its properties in the property sheet.

All forms and their controls have *properties* which allow you to change their size, shape, font, color and many other facets of their appearance or behavior. For a full description of all the properties, see Access Help. In this example we are going to change the background color of the Northwind Orders form.

1 Open the form in design view and, if it's not there already, bring up the Property sheet by clicking the **Properties** button on the Form Design toolbar

2 Click on a blank region of the design grid, so that the property sheet focuses on the form "Detail" area

3 Click on the "Back Color" property and then on the little button to the right of it

4 Select a color from the range shown

5 Run the form by selecting the **View > Form** menu option and observe how the background color has changed

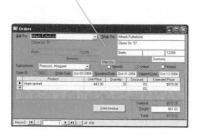

Adding a Calculated Control

A calculated control contains a value which it derives from other sources. In this example we're going to create a form that lets a user select a product from the underlying Products table, then enter the quantity required in a unbound textbox. We're going to display the total cost of the user's purchase using a calculated textbox control.

We've started with a database, into which we have imported the Northwind Products table (see Chapter 5). We have created a form that is bound to the table and includes two controls bound to the "Product Name" and "Unit Price" fields which we added using the Field List (see p. 87-88).

It's always a good idea to give controls you create meaningful names, rather than the default ones Access creates. To change the name of a control, change its Name property in the Property sheet.

We have also added two unbound text controls from the toolbox, one called "Quantity" and the other called "TotalValue".

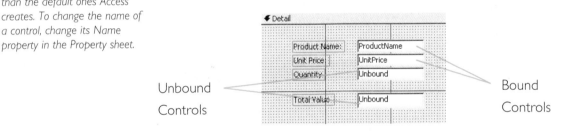

Unbound Controls

Bound Controls

Surround control names with square brackets "[ ]" otherwise Access thinks they are field names.

In the Control Source property of the TotalValue control, we have entered an *expression*, which multiplies the value in the "Unit Price" control by the value in the "Quantity" control:

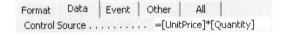

You can use the Expression Builder (see Access Help) to help you put these expressions together. It also lists all the special functions like date, time and aggregation that you can use in your own expressions.

Note that we prefix this expression with an equals sign, otherwise Access will assume it is a field name and not a calculated control. We change the TotalValue textbox's Format property to Currency so that it displays the result as a monetary amount.

Run the form, enter a quantity and observe the total value update accordingly. Change quantities and move from record to record and see the Total Value change each time.

Changing a Form's Appearance

To change a form's appearance you need to be in Design View. Click on the form and select the **View > Design View** menu option or click on the **View** toolbar button and select "Design View".

Resizing an Object

Hold down the CTRL key to select multiple controls, or "draw" an area with the mouse that encloses the controls you want to work with.

Click on the object you wish to resize and little black squares appear, surrounding it. These are call *resize handles.* Click on one (the cursor changes to a double-headed arrow) and drag. When you release the mouse button, the object will be resized.

Resize handles

To delete a control, simply click on it to bring up the resize handles, then press the DELETE key.

Moving an Object

Select the object by clicking it and the resize handles appear. Move the mouse over the control until the cursor changes into a little hand symbol. Then click the left mouse button and hold it down to move the object. Release the mouse button to "drop" the object into a new position.

Using AutoFormat

When using AutoFormats, choose the Edit > Select All menu option first, otherwise your formatting will only be applied to the control that has the focus.

Access has a number of built-in themes that you can use to customize the appearance of forms and controls.

1 Click the **AutoFormat** button on the Form Design toolbar

All formatting options can also be set in the Format tab of the control's Property sheet.

2 Select the style you require and click **OK**

3 Run the form to see the changes

Changing the Tab Order of Forms

Changing the form's tab order won't change it's appearance. It merely changes the order you visit the fields when you use the TAB key to move between them.

You can use the TAB key for moving between fields when entering or modifying data. You might decide to enter the information in a different order, or the tab order might be altered when you add a new control to your form. Here we show you how to change the form's tab order. Open the form in Design View and then follow the steps below.

1 Select the **View > Tab Order** menu option

2 In the dialog box, click on the field whose position in the tab order you want to change

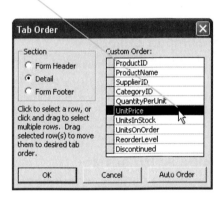

*If you want Access to reorder for you in a simple left-to-right and top-to-bottom fashion, click on **Auto Order.***

3 Holding down the left mouse button, "drag" it to its new position in the list and release it

4 Click on **OK** to finalize the tab order for the form

Creating List and Combo Boxes

It's often a good idea to force the user to select the value they want to enter into a field from a list. This makes data entry much faster and is also more accurate, because there is less danger of mistyping the entry.

There are two controls in Access ideally suited to this task: List boxes and Combo boxes.

List Boxes

List box values are always visible and the user is limited to choosing a value from the list. They are best used when there are only a handful of values to choose from.

Combo Boxes

A combo box occupies the same amount of space as a standard text box until you click on its down arrow. Then you're presented with a list of values to choose from. You can type in values that aren't in the list (unless the "Limit To List" property is set to "Yes").

Using the List/Combo Box Wizard

1   Make sure the toolbox **Control Wizard** button is pressed

2   Select the control (List or Combo box) from the toolbox

Combo Box   List Box

The same wizard runs whether you are creating a list box or a combo box, even though we're showing screenshots for a list box here.

3 Click on the form's design grid to place the control and the Wizard starts:

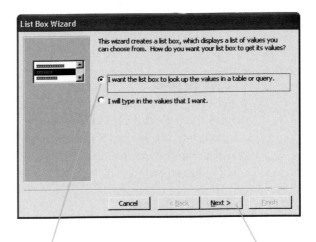

4 Do you want the Combo/List Box to derive its information from a table, or type in the values yourself?

5 Click **Next** and depending what choice you made, rejoin the text at the appropriate point below

Creating a List/Combo Box to Lookup Values in a Table or Query

6 On the next page of the wizard, select the Table or Query that you want the list/combo box to get its information from and click **Next**

Use whatever fields you want your users to see, but include the primary key field so that Access can uniquely identify the record that the user selected.

7 Select the fields you want the list/combo box to display; use the arrow buttons to move fields from "Available" to "Selected" (and back again if you make a mistake!)

8 Click **Next**

9 Click here to specify a field that the list of values should be sorted on

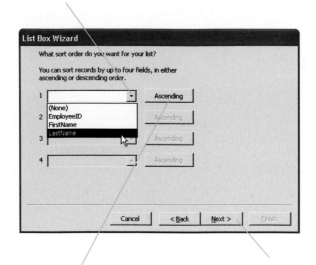

10 Click the button to toggle the sort order (ascending or descending)

11 Click **Next**

12 Check the box to hide the primary key field

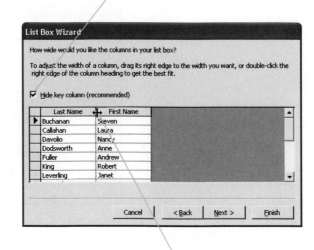

13 Click between the columns, hold down and "drag" to resize

|4 Click **Next**

|5 Give your list/combo box a meaningful name and click **Finish**

|6 Run the form. Your list/combo box is populated by values from your table or query

Creating a List/Combo Box Based on Typed Values

6 Specify the number of columns you want

7 Type the values

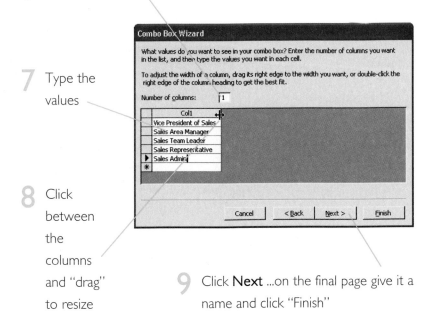

8 Click between the columns and "drag" to resize

9 Click **Next** ...on the final page give it a name and click "Finish"

About Subforms

A subform is just "a form within a form".

A subform is a "form within a form" which displays data related to the record currently being viewed in the main form. When the record changes in the main form, the data in the subform changes too.

Here's an example from the Northwind database. This is the "Quarterly Orders" form.

Data about the customer in the main form. When the user moves to another record, she will be looking at another customer's details

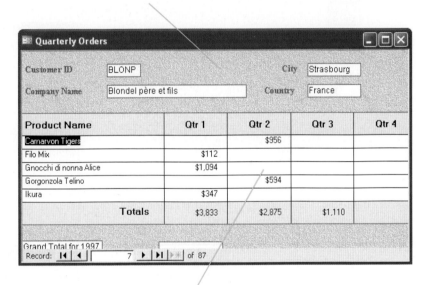

For each customer, the subform shows details of the orders they have placed in the year, by quarter

Typically you'll create the main form and subform together at design time. But Access also lets you:

- Create a subform and add it to an existing form

- Add one form to another to create a form with a subform

- Create a form with two or more subforms

- Create subforms within other subforms

Creating a Subform

To make an existing form the subform of another existing form, first open up the main form in the Design view. Then follow the steps below:

Before attempting to add the subform, ensure that the Control Wizards button in the toolbox is lit:

1 Click the Subform/Subreport button in the toolbox

2 "Draw" the subform on the design grid using the cursor

3 Access launches the subform wizard. Select "Use an existing form" and highlight the form you want to use as a subform

4 Click **Next**

5 Specify how the main form and subform are linked

6 Click **Next**

7 On the next page of the wizard give the subform a name and click **Finish**. Run the form, use the navigation buttons to move between records and watch the subform update accordingly

Queries

We've seen how you can use the datasheet and forms to filter and sort records, but a far more powerful and flexible way of manipulating data is to use Queries. In this Chapter we'll teach you how to create, modify and use queries to give you full control over your data.

Covers

Chapter Seven

Creating a Query Using the Wizard

The most common type of query and the one we're going to be creating here is the *select* query. A select query selects records based on criteria you supply. Using the Query Wizard you choose which tables or queries to include and specify the conditions for selecting records. The wizard displays a datasheet containing any records in your source data that fulfil those criteria. You can modify the query later on in Design view if you want to be more specific about the type of data it returns.

1 Switch to the Queries pane in the database window

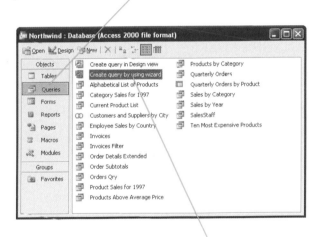

2 Double click on the "Create query by using wizard" link

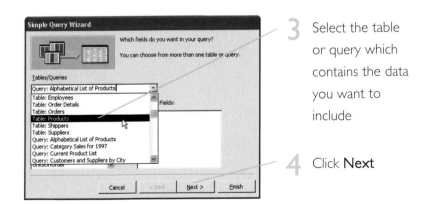

3 Select the table or query which contains the data you want to include

4 Click **Next**

...cont'd

You can use the bottom arrow buttons to deselect any fields you've included in error.

*You can include fields from more than one table or query. Just click "Back" to return to the first page of the wizard, select another data source and then click **Next** to include its fields.*

When you build your own queries, you might want to see totals or an average instead of individual records. Use the summary option on this page of the wizard for this.

5 Use the arrow buttons to move the fields you want to include into the list of "Selected Fields"

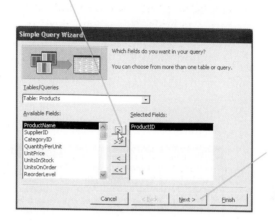

6 Repeat steps 3-5 until you have included all your fields

7 Click **Next**

8 If the wizard asks you if you want a "Detail" or "Summary" report (which it will only do if you have chosen numerical fields), select "Detail" and click **Next**

9 On the final page of the wizard, enter a name for your query and click **Finish**

10 Access creates the query based on your criteria and displays the data it has found in a datasheet

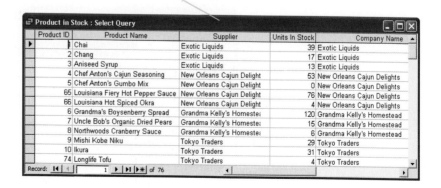

Creating a Query in the Design View

You also have the option of building your query from scratch, in the Design View. Once you are proficient at building queries, you'll find this method gives you the greatest flexibility. Don't neglect the wizard though – it helps to get something working quickly which you can then modify to suit your purposes.

Follow these steps to create a simple select query from scratch.

1   Go the Queries pane of the Database Window

2   Double click on "Create query in Design view"

Queries can get their data from other queries as well as tables.

3   Select the table or query that you want to include

5   Your data sources appear in the Design view

4   Click **Add**

6 When you have finished adding your data sources, click the **Close** button in the Show Table dialog box

You can drag fields from the field list to the design grid, if you prefer.

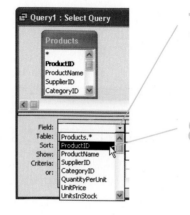

7 Click in the Field box in the bottom half of the Query Design Window and click on the arrow that appears

Clicking on the asterisk at the top of the field list selects all the fields in that table.

8 Select the first field you want to include from the drop-down list

9 Move along to the next column of the Design view to continue adding fields until you have selected all the fields you require

Don't forget to save all your hard work!

10 Select the **File > Save** menu option and in the dialog box that appears, type a name for your query and click **OK**

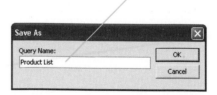

11 The query is saved and can be seen in the Database Window

12 To see the query in action, double click on its name in the database window, or click the **Run** button on the toolbar

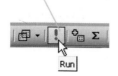

Querying on an Exact Match

Often, you'll want to see all the records that satisfy one particular condition. Here we're going to be using a query to list all the employees in the Northwind database who live in London.

1   Create a query that lists all the records in the Employees table, using either the wizard or the Design view (see p.100-103)

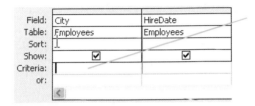

2   Find the field in the design view you want to specify criteria for and click in the cell in its "Criteria" row.

3   Type "London" in the query field (don't worry about the quotes, Access adds these automatically)

4   Click the **Save** button on the toolbar to save the query

5   Click the **Run** button on the toolbar to run the query

6   Access displays the results

	Last Name	First Name	Title	Region	City	Hire Date
▶	Buchanan	Steven	Sales Manager		London	Oct-17-2004
	Suyama	Michael	Sales Representative		London	Oct-17-2004
	King	Robert	Sales Representative		London	Jan-02-2004
	Dodsworth	Anne	Sales Representative		London	Nov-02-2004
*						

Querying on a Range of Matches

Instead of an exact condition you can specify a range of conditions to tell Access which records to include. In this example, we're going to list all the items in the Products table that cost $45 or more. We can use the mathematical "greater than or equals" operator (">=") in the criteria cell to achieve this.

1 Create a query that lists all the records in the Products table, using either the wizard or the Design view (see p. 100-103)

2 Type ">=45" (no quotes or currency sign) in the Criteria cell of the Unit Price field

Field:	ProductName	UnitPrice
Table:	Products	Products
Sort:		
Show:	☑	☑
Criteria:		>=45
or:		

3 Save the query, then run it

4 Access displays all the products where the Unit Price is equal to or greater than $45

Product Name	Unit Price
Mishi Kobe Niku	$97.00
Carnarvon Tigers	$62.50
Sir Rodney's Marmalade	$81.00
Rössle Sauerkraut	$45.60
Thüringer Rostbratwurst	$123.79
Côte de Blaye	$263.50
Ipoh Coffee	$46.00
Manjimup Dried Apples	$53.00
Raclette Courdavault	$55.00
Tarte au sucre	$49.30
	$0.00

Expensive Products : Select Query

Record: ◄◄ ◄ 1 ► ►► ►* of 10

Using Multiple Data Sources

Data can come from other queries, as well as tables.

Often you'll want to bring together data from more than one source in your query. For example, the Northwind Products table is linked to the Categories table by the Category ID field. If you want to list the Products along with their categories then you'll need to look up the Category Name for each ID in the Categories table, otherwise all you'll have is a number which will be meaningless to you and your users.

All you need to do is include both tables when you create the query. The link between them will ensure that each Products record has a match in the Categories table, so then it's just a matter of selecting the right fields.

I   We have included both the Products and Categories tables so we can have each product's details as well as its Category Name

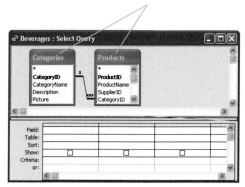

2   We can now choose to include fields from either table

Field:	ProductName	CategoryName
Table:	Products	Categories
Sort:		
Show:	☑	☑
Criteria:		Beverages
or:		

Querying on Multiple Criteria

You may wish to select records that match more than one criterion. For example, you might want to include Products that are *either* beverages, seafood or condiments.

To do this, you use the **OR** operator.

1 Start with your single criteria (which you learned how to do in "Querying on an Exact Match" on p. 104)

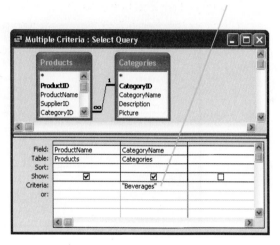

2 Enter the other values that you want to match in the "OR" rows for that column

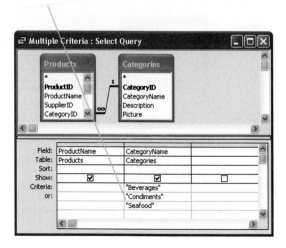

Matching on Multiple Fields

In some queries, you'll want the record to satisfy several conditions before it is included. These are often called **AND** queries, because the data needs to match the first criterion *and* any subsequent ones.

For instance, if you wish to include any German confectionery items in the Products table that cost more than $20:

Always test your queries thoroughly to make sure that they are returning the right data otherwise you might find yourself making decisions based upon inadequate information!

Enter each separate criterion in the correct column for that field

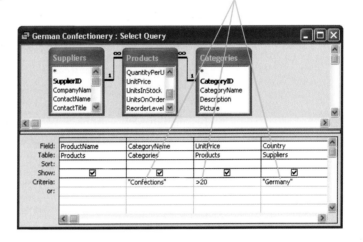

For more information about queries, consult Access Help.

Access includes only those records that fulfill *all* the criteria

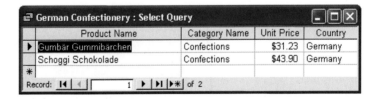

The Query Design View is a powerful tool, allowing you to produce highly complex queries using multiple criteria and data sources with just a few mouse clicks.

The best way to learn how to use it is to practise! Define your query, run it and see if the resulting data is what you were expecting!

Changing the Display of Query Results

Sorting Records Within a Query

Access lets you specify the sort order of the records in your query.

You can sort on more than one field, such as by department and then surname.

Access sorts in the order the fields are listed in the Design view.

1 Click in the Sort row underneath the field you want to sort the information by and a down arrow appears

Field:	ProductName	UnitPrice
Table:	Products	Products
Sort:		
Show:	☑	☑
Criteria:		>=45
or:		

2 Click on the down arrow and select Ascending or Descending

Field:	ProductName	UnitPrice
Table:	Products	Products
Sort:		
Show:	Ascending	☑
Criteria:	Descending	>=45
or:	(not sorted)	

3 Save and run the query and the records are listed in the order you specified

Expensive Products : Select Query	
Product Name	**Unit Price**
Carnarvon Tigers	$62.50
Côte de Blaye	$263.50
Ipoh Coffee	$46.00
Manjimup Dried Apples	$53.00
Mishi Kobe Niku	$97.00
Raclette Courdavault	$55.00
Rössle Sauerkraut	$45.60
Sir Rodney's Marmalade	$81.00
Tarte au sucre	$49.30
Thüringer Rostbratwurst	$123.79
*	$0.00

Record: ◄◄ ◄ | 1 | ► ►► ►* of 10

Hiding Fields

See the example on the next page.

Sometimes you'll want to include a field in your query design, but keep it hidden when you display the query results, such as when it's already known (e.g. a query that selects all widgets where color = blue).

Click here to toggle between hiding/showing the field

ProductSales: ExtendedPrice	OrderDate
Order Details Extended	Orders
Sum	Where
☑	☐
	Between #1/1/2004# And #12/31/2004#

Adding and Removing Fields

Adding a Field to the Query

1 In Design view, click on the field you want to add in the list of fields and hold the left mouse button down

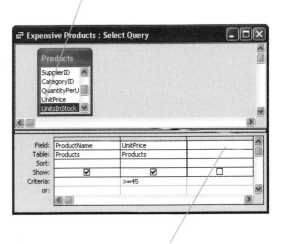

2 "Drag" it to an empty column in the design grid and release the left mouse button to add the field

Removing a Field From the Query

1 Click on the bar above the field entries to select the field

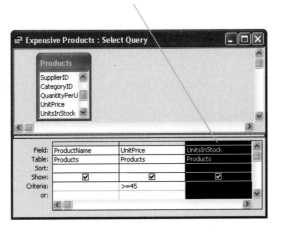

2 Press the DELETE key

Creating a Make-Table Query

Queries that make changes to the underlying data are called "Action Queries".

See p. 112.

So far we have been looking at "Select" queries. Another type of query is a **Make-Table Query**, which as its name suggests creates a new table based on query results. In our example we're going to create a new table which we'll call "Seafood" which contains just the seafood items in the Products table.

1 We start off with a select query that includes only those records that we're going to put in the new table

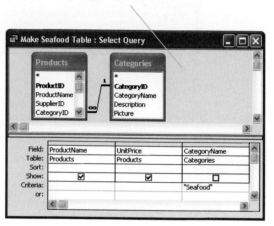

2 Select "Make-Table Query" from the Query menu

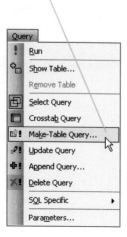

3 Give the new table a name

4 Click **OK**

If you don't get this warning, follow the steps described in "About Action Queries" below.

5 Save and Run the query

6 Access tells you that it is going to create a new table and add a specified number of rows (records)

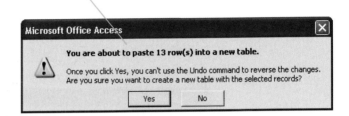

7 Click **Yes** to continue

8 Access creates a new table which is now visible in the Database Window and contains the data your query has selected

About Action Queries

A Make-Table Query is an example of an *action query*. An action query is a query that makes changes to or moves many records in just one operation. There are three other types of action query: Delete, Update and Append.

When you run an action query, Access should ask for your approval before making the changes, as in Step 6 above. You can turn this behavior on and off from the **Tools > Options** menu. In the Edit/Find tab, simply put a check in the "Action Queries" check box.

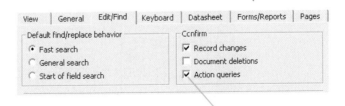

Place a check in this check box to turn warnings on

Creating a Delete Query

You can also use a query to handle the bulk deletion of records according to specified criteria.

1 Start with a query that includes the fields you want to search, but which does not contain any criteria

Field:	ProductName	UnitPrice	CategoryName
Table:	Product List	Product List	Product List
Sort:			
Show:	☑	☑	☑
Criteria:			
or:			

Take care with your delete queries – once data has been deleted it's gone for good!

2 Select the **Query > Delete Query** menu option

3 A separate "Delete" row appears. In the row beneath it enter the criteria for the records you want to delete. Here we're going to delete all the products in the "Beverages" category

Make a select query to test your criteria and only turn it into a delete query when you're sure that it's picking up the right records.

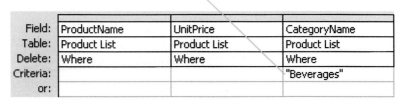

Field:	ProductName	UnitPrice	CategoryName
Table:	Product List	Product List	Product List
Delete:	Where	Where	Where
Criteria:			"Beverages"
or:			

4 Save and run the query

5 Access warns that records are going to be deleted – click on the "Yes" button

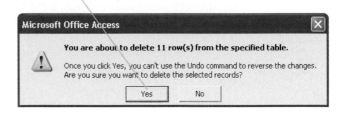

Microsoft Office Access

You are about to delete 11 row(s) from the specified table.

Once you click Yes, you can't use the Undo command to reverse the changes. Are you sure you want to delete the selected records?

[Yes] [No]

Creating an Update Query

You can use an update query to handle the bulk update of records. In this example we're going to impose a 10% price increase on all our products.

1 Start with a query that includes the fields you want to search, but which does not contain any criteria

Field:	ProductName	UnitPrice	CategoryName
Table:	Product List	Product List	Product List
Sort:			
Show:	☑	☑	☑
Criteria:			
or:			

2 Select the **Query > Update Query** menu option

Access has a useful tool called the "Expression Builder" which helps you piece together your own expressions. Consult Access Help.

3 Enter a value or expression for the fields you want to update – here we are multiplying the value of the UnitPrice field by 1.1 to effect a 10% increase in the price of each product

Field:	ProductName	UnitPrice	CategoryName
Table:	Product List	Product List	Product List
Update To:		[UnitPrice]*1.1	
Criteria:			
or:			

4 Save and run the query

5 Access warns that records are going to be modified – click on the **Yes** button to accept these changes. Look at the entries in the source table to verify that they have been changed appropriately

Creating an Append Query

Append queries are used for adding records from one or more source tables to the end of a single destination table. In this simple example we have some new products in our "New Products" table that we want to add to our "Product List" table.

1 Start with a query that includes the fields you want to add from the source table (in this case, "New Products")

2 Select the **Query > Append Query** menu option and select the table you want to append these records to

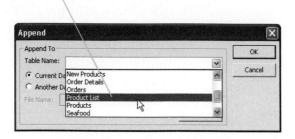

Although the fields can be named differently in the source and destination tables, they must be of a compatible data type.

3 If the source and destination fields have different names, then you need to change the names of the destination fields in the "Append To" row

Field:	ProductName	UnitPrice	CategoryName
Table:	New Products	New Products	New Products
Sort:			
Append To:	ProductName	UnitPrice	CategoryName
Criteria:			
or:			

4 Enter any criteria in the usual way if you only want to append certain records from the source table

5 Save and run the query and click **Yes** to append the records to the new table

Creating "Special" Queries

As well as the Simple Query Wizard that we used at the beginning of this chapter, Access also has wizards for three other "special" queries: the "Find Duplicates" wizard, the "Find Unmatched" wizard and the "Crosstab" wizard. To start these wizards, click the "New" button in the Queries pane of the Database Window and select the one you want from the list.

The Find Duplicates Wizard

The Find Duplicates Wizard shows all records with duplicate values in the field(s) you specify. Simply select the field in the wizard and let Access do the rest.

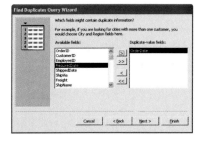

The Find Unmatched Wizard

The Find Unmatched Wizard displays all the records in one table that have no match in another, related table. You use the wizard to select both tables and the fields that join them.

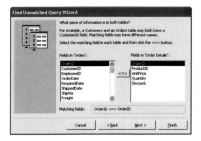

The Crosstab Query Wizard

The Crosstab Query Wizard helps you create queries that calculate sums, averages, counts or other totals that are grouped by two types of information: one down the left side of the datasheet (e.g. Customer) and another across the top (e.g. Sales by Quarter).

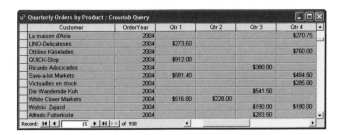

Customer	OrderYear	Qtr 1	Qtr 2	Qtr 3	Qtr 4
La maison d'Asie	2004				$270.75
LINO-Delicateses	2004	$273.60			
Ottilies Käseladen	2004				$760.00
QUICK-Stop	2004	$912.00			
Ricardo Adocicados	2004			$380.00	
Save-a-lot Markets	2004	$581.40			$484.50
Victuailles en stock	2004				$285.00
Die Wandernde Kuh	2004			$541.50	
White Clover Markets	2004	$516.80	$228.00		
Wolski Zajazd	2004			$190.00	$190.00
Alfreds Futterkiste	2004			$283.50	

Reports

You can use reports to create abstracts or summaries of your data. These can be printed out and distributed to other people or incorporated within other documents. Access provides a wizard and AutoReports for creating reports and we'll show you how these work first. Then we'll delve into the Design view where you can build new reports from scratch and modify existing ones. By the end of this chapter you should be able to create quite sophisticated reports that will impress your colleagues!

Covers

Chapter Eight

Creating a Report With the Wizard

Like the Form Wizard, using the Report Wizard is a great way of getting a report working quickly. You can always tweak it to your exact requirements later on. Follow these steps to create a simple report using the wizard.

Switch to the Reports pane in the database window

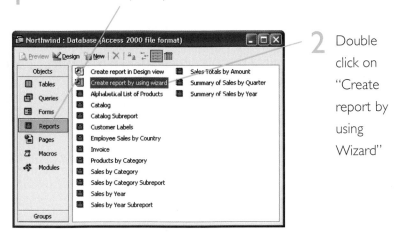

2 Double click on "Create report by using Wizard"

3 Select the table or query upon which to base your report

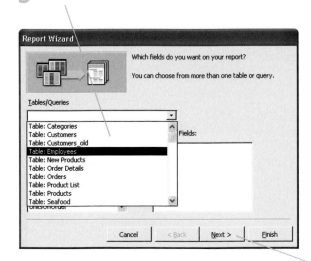

4 Click **Next**

5 Select the fields you want to include in your report by clicking on the arrows to move them from the "Available Fields" box to the "Selected Fields" box

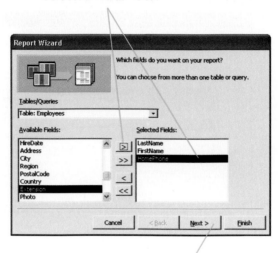

*You can always click the **Back** button to revisit the earlier stages of the wizard.*

6 When you have chosen your fields, click **Next**

7 On this page of the wizard you can specify grouping levels if you wish: we'll learn how to do this later in this chapter

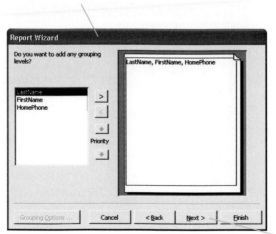

8 For now, click **Next**

You can sort by up to four fields. For example, you could sort by Department, Job Title, Surname and then First Name.

9 Optionally you can specify a sort order for the fields in your report – select the fields from the drop-down lists

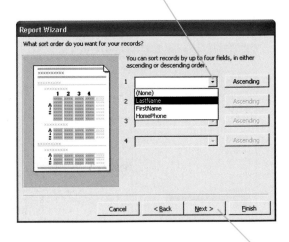

10 Click **Next**

11 By default, the sort order for each field is ascending, but you can toggle the sort order by clicking on the buttons

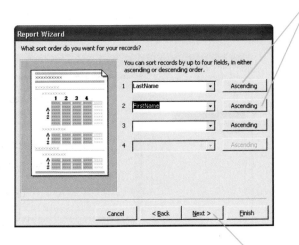

12 Click **Next**

13 Access gives you a choice of standard layouts – click the radio button for the one you wish to use

You can change the orientation of your report here too. If your report contains a lot of fields you may wish to turn the page on its side with the "Landscape" option.

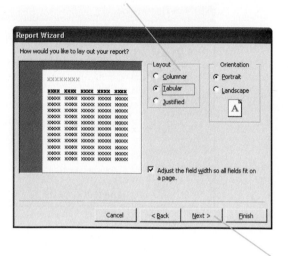

14 Click **Next**

15 Select a style for your report

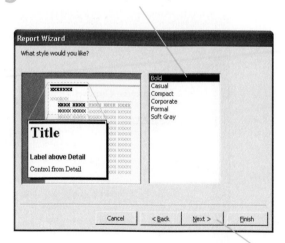

16 Click **Next**

Access automatically saves the report, using a file name based on the title you supply here.

17 Give your report a title

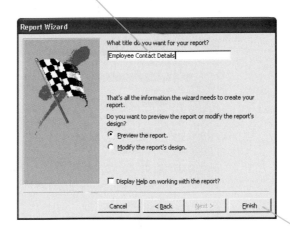

18 Click **Finish**

19 Access displays the finished report

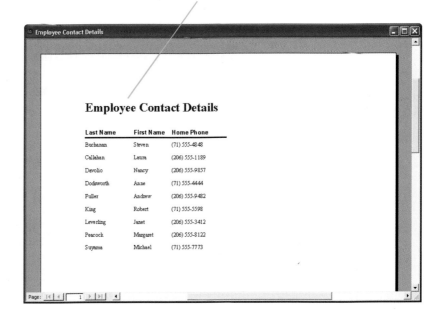

Creating a Report Using AutoReports

You can also use *AutoReports* to create a variety of reports. This method is even quicker than the wizard. Start in the Reports pane of the database window and follow these steps.

1 Click on the **New** button in the Database Window

2 Select the report layout (columnar or tabular)

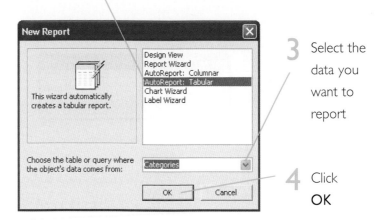

3 Select the data you want to report

4 Click **OK**

Unlike the wizard, an AutoReport does not automatically save the report.

5 Access displays the report

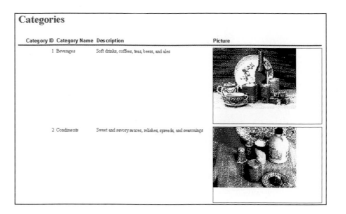

Saving a Report

As with everything else you create using Access, you must remember to save your reports. Access will prompt you if you attempt to close a report without saving it first, but it is important to get into the habit of saving your work regularly.

For every menu option there is usually an equivalent button on the toolbar.

1 Open the File menu and click **Save**

2 If the report is a new one, Access will ask you to enter a name for it. Type it in and click **OK**

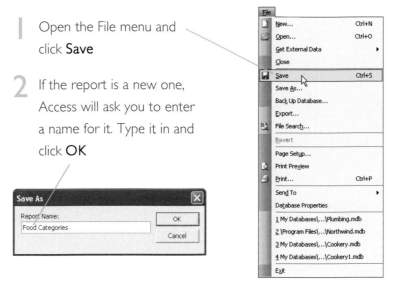

3 Access saves the report and you can now see it in the Reports pane of the Database Window

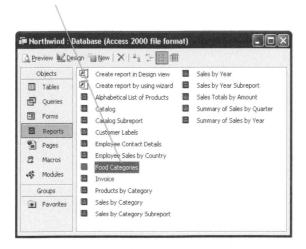

Opening a Report

To open a specific report, first make sure you have opened the database that report belongs to. Then:

1 Click the **Reports** option in the Objects bar

2 Double click on the report you want to use

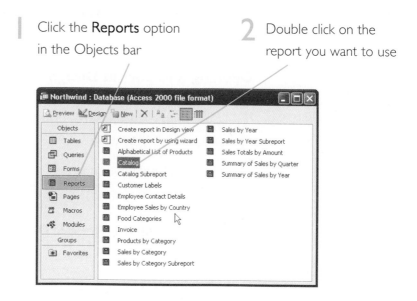

3 Access opens the report

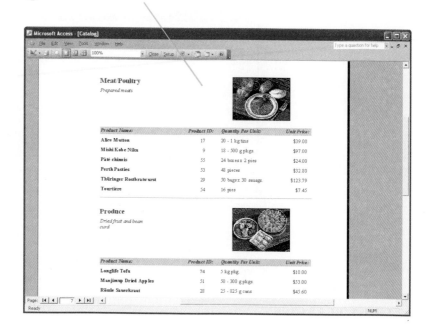

Looking at Reports in the Design View

Designing reports is very similar to designing forms. If you are familiar with the concepts we discussed in Chapter 6, you'll find designing reports a snap!

Whether you want to create a new report from scratch, or change some of the features of a report you have created using the wizard or an AutoReport, you'll need to learn how to manipulate it in the Design view. The Report Design View is very similar to the Form Design View, which we covered in chapter 6. If you've mastered forms, then reports will be a breeze.

Opening a Report in Design View

1 In the Database Window's Reports pane, click on the report you want to modify or view

2 Click the **Design** button in the Database Window toolbar

Components of the Report Design View

Report Design Toolbar   Report & Page Headers   Field List

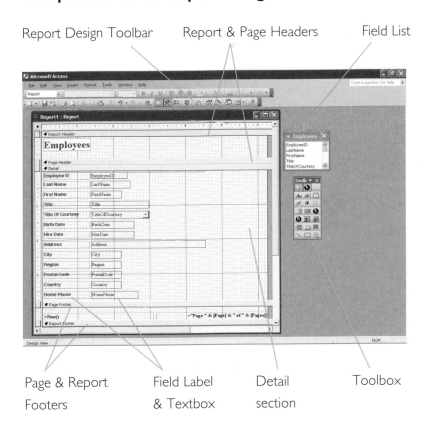

Page & Report Footers   Field Label & Textbox   Detail section   Toolbox

Working With Report Controls

Just like forms (see chapter 6), a report contains *controls*. Controls include labels to provide descriptive data and text boxes which display information from the underlying data source.

Selecting a Control

Click on a control to select it. Moving and sizing handles appear. Some labels are bound to the text box they describe and appear together, as in the example below:

To remove a control, select it and press the DELETE key. If you make a mistake and want to restore the control, click on the Edit > Undo menu option.

Label   Text Box

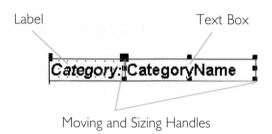

Moving and Sizing Handles

Moving and Resizing Controls

To *move* a control, simply click within the area bound by the little black squares. The cursor changes into a little hand symbol:

Hand cursor

"Drag" the control to the new position by holding down the left mouse button. Release the button at the point where you wish to place it.

To *resize* a control, move the mouse cursor over one of the handles and it will change to a double-headed arrow:

Arrow cursor

Click and hold down the left mouse button and "drag" the handle. Release the mouse button to resize the control.

Creating a New Report From Scratch

Creating a New Report in Design View

Follow the steps below to start building a new report in the Design view.

1 Click the **New** button in the Database Window's toolbar

2 Select the "Design View" option

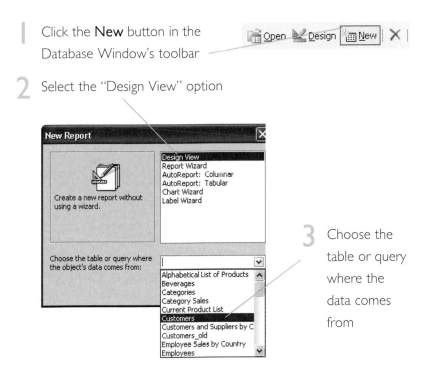

3 Choose the table or query where the data comes from

Changing the Page Layout

You might wish to change the orientation of your page, size of the paper it will be printed on, or the margins. You can do all this from the **File > Page Setup** menu option.

- In the **Margins** tab, specify the amount of blank space to be left around the edges of the page

- In the **Pages** tab, select the page orientation. "Landscape" turns the page on its side and is useful when you are including a lot of fields in your report. Select the paper size and specify the printer in this tab too

- In the **Columns** tab you can divide the printed area into columns for a more sophisticated presentation

Report and Page Headers and Footers

Structure of a Report

The detail section is the part that usually displays the data. It is repeated for each record. As well as the detail section we can use report and page headers and footers.

Access makes it easy to add page numbering and automatic dates to your report. Simply select what you need from the *Insert* menu.

- The **report header** appears once at the beginning of a report and is the first thing Access prints. It is therefore suitable for a logo, report title or similar

- The **page header** appears at the top of every page and is typically used for column headings

- The **page footer** appears at the bottom of every page and is often used for page numbers

- The **report footer** appears once at the end of the report. You use it to display final items such as report totals. The report footer is the last section in the Report Design View but is nevertheless printed *before* the page footer on the last page of the report

When you create a report in the design view, the page header and footer are shown by default. To view the report header and footer, select the **View > Report Header/Footer** menu option.

Resizing Headers and Footers

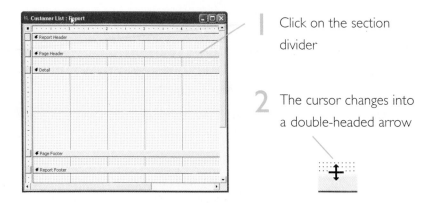

1 Click on the section divider

2 The cursor changes into a double-headed arrow

3 Hold down the left mouse button and "drag" the divider to resize the section; release when at the desired size

Adding a Label to the Report

You can use a label for your report title. But labels aren't just used in titles – a label is useful anwhere descriptive information is required and the process for creating one is exactly the same wherever you are.

*If you can't see the toolbox, click on the **View** > **Toolbox** menu option.*

1 Open the report in Design view

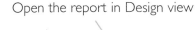

2 Click the **Label** button in the toolbox

3 The cursor changes to a letter "A" with a plus symbol

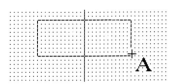

4 Click and "drag" to draw the boundary box for the label on the design grid

You can also change label text by modifying the label's Caption property.

5 When you release the mouse button, Access waits for you to type in the text for the label

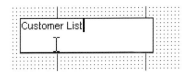

6 Run the report by clicking on the **View** button – Access displays the label with the text you typed

Adding Fields to the Report

Adding fields to your report (like most operations in the Report Design View) is very similar to adding fields to a form, just like we did in Chapter 6.

1 Open the report in Design view

2 Ensure that the "Field List" box is visible – if not, you can bring it up by clicking the **Field List** button on the "Report Design" toolbar

3 Select the field(s) you want on your form (hold down the CTRL key to select multiple fields)

The label name is derived from the name of the underlying field. To change it, click on the label and type a new name.

4 "Drag" the field from the field box across to your form design

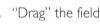

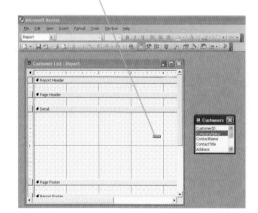

As you can see here, the label name is too long and does not display properly. Click on the label and hover the mouse over the top left handle until the cursor changes to a pointing finger. You can then move the label independently of the field and reposition or resize it as you wish.

5 Access places the field on your form together with a descriptive label

Changing the Report's Appearance

Using Toolbox Graphics

You can use graphical elements in the toolbox to make your reports look more professional. One useful tool is the Line tool, which can be used as a separator between text items for a clearer display.

If you can't see the toolbox, bring it up by clicking on the Toolbox icon on the Report Design toolbar.

I   Click on the **Line** tool in the toolbox

2   "Draw" the line on your report design by "dragging" the cursor – release it when you're done

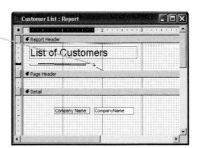

3   View the report to see your handiwork in action

Setting Control Properties

Like form controls (see Chapter 6), report controls each have a property sheet associated with them where you can make changes to modify their behavior and appearance. Most of the options relating to appearance are located in the "Format" tab:

1 Click on the report control in Design view

2 If the property sheet is not already visible, click on the Properties toolbar button

Properties

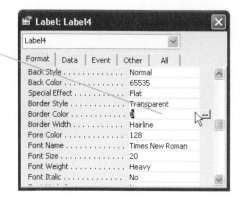

3 Type (or select) the new value for the property in the Properties window

If you don't see the properties you're expecting to see, you might not have selected the right control or report element. Click on the control or report area to see the properties for that particular element.

Properties that you can use to dynamically alter the appearance of your reports include Font Name, Font Size, Back Color and Fore Color (for background and foreground color respectively). As well as selecting the properties for individual controls, you can also make changes to several controls at once (where those controls have common properties), by either "drawing" an area with the mouse around the controls you want to change, or by holding down the CTRL key and clicking on them.

You can also make changes to report sections, or to the report as a whole. For instance, to change the background color of the Detail section:

1 Click on the Detail section header to select this part of the report

2 Switch to the Format tab (if required) and click on the right hand column for the "Back Color" property

3 Access displays a choice of colors – select one, then click on the form to see the change

Using AutoFormats

If you want to a quick and easy way to change the appearance of your report, then use an AutoFormat. AutoFormats offer a range of styles which can be applied to your entire report, saving you the trouble of configuring sections, controls and other objects individually.

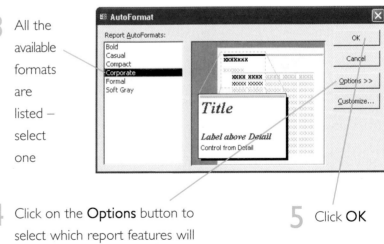

1 Click in the top left hand corner to select the entire report

2 Select the **Format > AutoFormat** menu option

Access allows you to change existing AutoFormats and create new ones. Click on the **Customize** *button and consult Access Help for more details.*

3 All the available formats are listed – select one

4 Click on the **Options** button to select which report features will be affected by AutoFormat

5 Click **OK**

6 Run the report to see the changes

Adding a Picture

Follow the steps below to include a picture in your report, such as a company logo or illustration:

If you put the image in the detail section it will appear alongside every record in the finished report. It's usual therefore to place pictures in the header or footer sections.

1   Click the section of the report where you want to place the image (header, detail, footer, etc)

2   Select the **Picture** option from the Insert menu

3   Click on the picture you want in your report

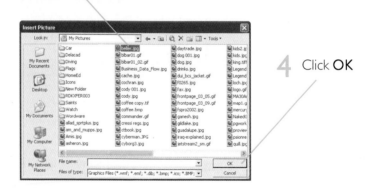

4   Click **OK**

Once the image has been placed you can move, resize or delete it like any other report control (see p. 127).

5   Access places the picture on the report

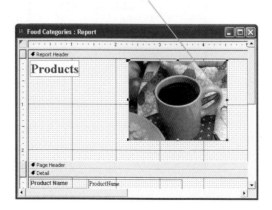

Sorting and Grouping Report Data

You can sort and group records based on the values in one or more fields, allowing you to present your data in a way that makes for easy analysis. Although the wizard guides you through the sorting and grouping options, it's also possible to do this yourself in Design view as we shall demonstrate here. In this example, we are creating a report that lists Customers by the country in which they are based.

First, open the report in Design view and select the **View >**
Sorting and Grouping menu option

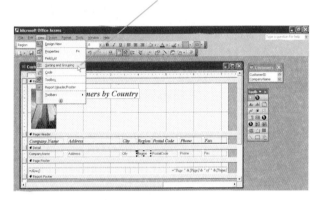

2 Select the field(s) you wish to group by from the list

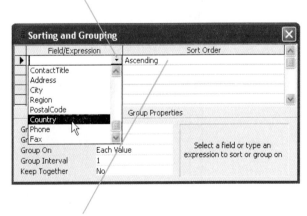

3 Select the sort order for the field (ascending by default)

4 Choose whether to display a group header or footer for the report – click on the appropriate field and then on the down arrow for a list of options

Group footers are a good place to include subtotals. You implement these like calculated controls in forms. See p. 140.

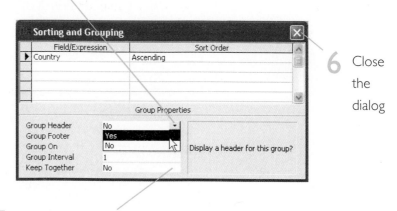

6 Close the dialog

With "Whole Group", the header, footer and all detail records are kept on the same page. The "With First Detail" option ensures that the group header is only printed if at least one detail record can fit on the page after it.

5 To keep the group together, without any page breaks, click here and then on the down arrow and select either "Whole Group" or "With First Detail"

7 If you chose to have a group header or footer (step 4 above), Access adds a new section to the report

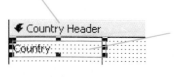

The easiest way to add new fields is by using the Field List. See p. 131.

8 We've added a new field to this section, to display the country for each group

9 Save and run the report to see the grouping at work

Company Name	Address	City	Region	Postal Code	Phone
Argentina					
Océano Atlántico L	Ing. Gustavo Moncada 8585	Buenos		1010	(1) 135-5333
Rancho grande	Av. del Libertador 900	Buenos		1010	(1) 123-5555
Cactus Comidas pa	Cerrito 333	Buenos		1010	(1) 135-5555
Austria					
Ernst Handel	Kirchgasse 6	Graz		8010	7675-3425
Piccolo und mehr	Geislweg 14	Salzburg		5020	6562-9722
Belgium					
Maison Dewey	Rue Joseph-Bens 532	Bruxelles		B-1180	(02) 201 24 67
Suprêmes délices	Boulevard Tirou, 255	Charleroi		B-6000	(071) 23 67 22

About Subreports

A subreport is a "report within a report". It displays further, related information about the data in the main body of the report. This is an example from the Northwind database, the "Sales by Year" report.

The subreport shows summary sales information for the year, on a quarterly basis

Sales by Year

Dec-01-2004

2004 Summary

Quarter:	Orders Shipped:	Sales:
4	18	$16,844
Totals:	18	$16,844

2004 Details

Line Number:	Shipped Date:	Order ID:	Sales:
1	Dec-13-2004	10376	$399
2	Dec-13-2004	10377	$864
3	Dec-14-2004	10379	$863
4	Dec-14-2004	10381	$112
5	Dec-14-2004	10382	$2,900
6	Dec-15-2004	10383	$899
7	Dec-15-2004	10378	$103
8	Dec-15-2004	10384	$2,222
9	Dec-16-2004	10387	$1,058
10	Dec-16-2004	10388	$1,229
11	Dec-17-2004	10385	$691
12	Dec-17-2004	10371	$73
13	Dec-17-2004	10389	$1,833

The main report shows all the individual orders that went towards making up the year's sales

With subreports you can: create a subreport and add it to an existing report; add one report to another to create a report with a subreport; create a report with two or more subreports; or create a subreport within another subreport.

Creating a Subreport

To make one existing report the subreport of another existing report, first open up the main report in the Design View. Then follow the steps below:

Before attempting to add the subreport, ensure that the **Control Wizards** *button in the toolbox is lit:*

1. Click the Subform/Subreport button in the toolbox

2. "Draw" the subreport on the design grid using the cursor

3. Access launches the subreport wizard. Select "Use an existing report" and highlight the report you want to use as a subreport

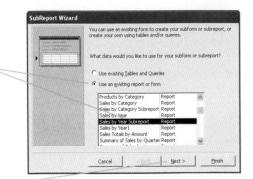

4. Click **Next**

6. Specify how the main report and subreport are linked

7. Click **Next**

8. On the next page of the wizard give the subreport a name and click **Finish**

Adding Totals and Counts

Adding a total or count to an Access report is very similar to adding a calculated field to a form, like we did in Chapter 6.

In our example, our report lists orders and their constituent items. We're going to include a field in our report which subtotals the value of each order.

1 Add a group footer to the report (see p. 137, Step 4)

For a grand total, put the total field in the report footer. Similarly, for a page total, put the field in the page footer. See p. 129 for a description of the various footer sections.

2 Add a field to the newly created group footer section, using the textbox control in the toolbox

3 In the properties sheet for the textbox, we enter an expression (using the Access SUM function) which totals the Value field

Because we want to display this total as a dollar amount, we've also specified that this number should be treated as a Currency value in the textbox's Format property.

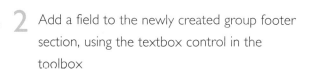

If you want a count, rather than a total, use the Access COUNT([Field Name]) function instead.

4 When we run the report we can see the subtotals

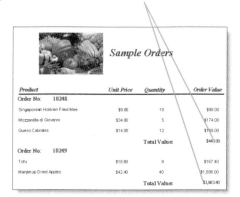

Previewing the Report

Before you print a report, it's often helpful to see how it will display on the page.

You can also double-click on the report to open it in preview mode.

1 Select the report you want to preview in the Reports pane of the database window

2 Click on the **Preview** button

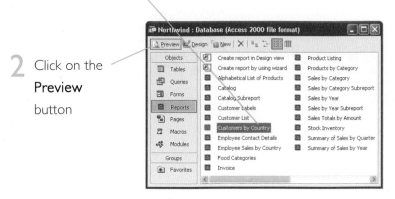

3 Access shows you how the report will look when it is printed:

Click on any area to see it in close-up

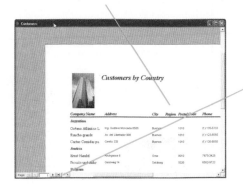

Click the page buttons to move to other pages in the report

Click the Two Pages or Multiple Pages buttons to see two, or several pages at once

Printing the Report

Having designed the report and seen a preview, you are now ready to print it out and distribute it.

1. Double-click on the report you want to print to open it

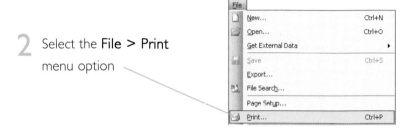

2. Select the **File > Print** menu option

3. Choose the Printer from the drop-down list

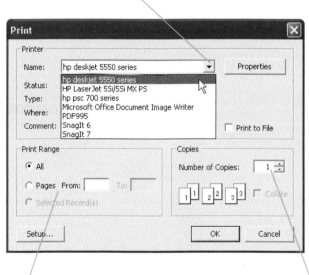

4. Select which pages to print (the default is "all")

5. Specify how many copies to print (the default is one)

6. Click **OK** and Access prints the report

Data Access Pages

Access 2003 makes it easy to share data over an intranet or on the World Wide Web, using *Data Access Pages*. In this chapter we'll explain exactly what Data Access Pages are, why you might want to use them and guide you through their creation. We'll show you how to group, summarize, edit, protect and ultimately publish your data to the Web.

Covers

Chapter Nine

About Data Access Pages

Very simply, a *Data Access Page* is a web page that is connected to an Access database. Data Access Pages let you share your data over an intranet or the World Wide Web. Users connect to the database via Internet Explorer and use it to search, edit and enter data.

To view your data access pages, your users need to have a valid Microsoft Office license and be running Internet Explorer v5.5 or later.

Data access pages can present data to users in a similar way to reports, but interactively. For example, you can *group* data together to give a summary view. If the user wants to "drill down" into more detailed information, they can expand these groups to see individual records and collapse them to get back to the summary view.

Click here to expand the view so you can see a list of all orders for 2004

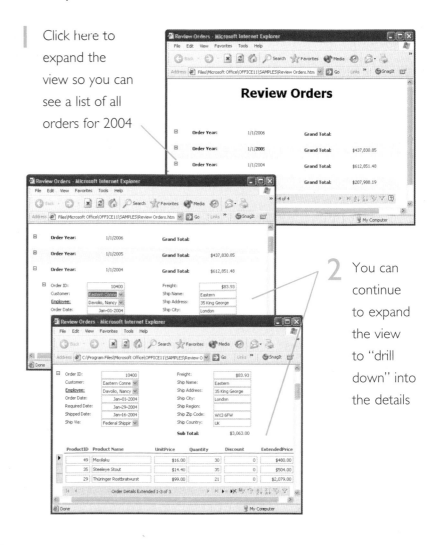

2 You can continue to expand the view to "drill down" into the details

Creating a Page Using AutoPage

AutoPages are the quickest way of getting your page up and running. The resulting page will be pretty basic, but it will give you a head start. We'll show you how to enhance the appearance of the page later in this chapter.

> In the **Pages** pane of the Database window, click on the **New** button

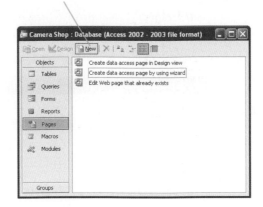

2 In the "New Data Access Page" dialog, choose "AutoReport: Columnar", select the query or table that will provide the underlying data and click **OK**

3 Access creates a new Page, which you should save using the **File > Save** menu option

You might see a message warning you that the connection string for the page is an absolute path. If you are connecting to the page via a network, you need to edit the connection string to include a UNC path. See Access Help for further details.

The Page that Access creates is very similar to a form or report. In fact, data access pages are really just a type of form or report suitable for viewing by a browser.

When you save the page, as in Step 3 above, Access creates a new page object which appears in the Database window. Additionally, it generates a HTML file for the page and a folder containing any associated graphics files. Unlike the page object, these are external to Access and are stored in the same directory as your database. Take care not to delete them, otherwise your pages won't work!

Creating a Page Using the Wizard

It's a good idea to start your page design with the wizard, because as well as giving you a head start, it takes away the complexity of certain aspects of page design, such as grouping.

Using the page wizard gives you a few more choices than the AutoPage method, including options for sorting and grouping records on the page.

1 Switch to the Pages pane in the database window

2 Click on the **New** button in the database window toolbar

3 Select Page Wizard

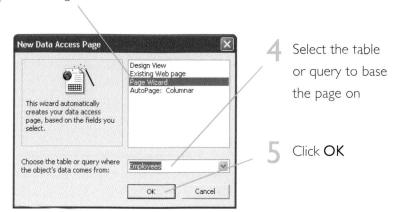

4 Select the table or query to base the page on

5 Click **OK**

6 Use the arrow buttons to select the fields in the underlying data (on the left hand side) you want to include on your page (on the right hand side)

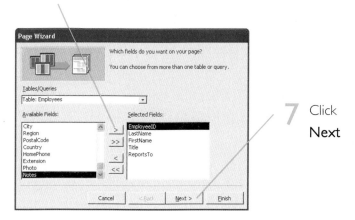

7 Click **Next**

8 In the next dialog box you can elect to group the data by certain fields. Select the group fields in the same way as Step 6. Here we're going to group by Region

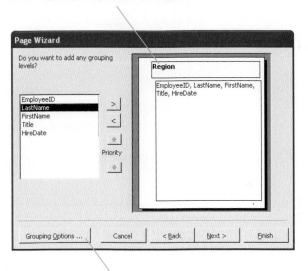

Grouping Intervals are a way in which you can "band" your data. For example, if you have a database of towns and cities, you might want to group by populations of 10,000. E.g. group 1 would be populations of 0-10,000, group 2 would be 10,000 to 20,000, and so on. Access gives you a choice of group intervals based on the type of data in the field you are grouping on.

9 If you want to specify a grouping interval for each of the fields you have chosen to group by, click here

10 In the next dialog box you can select a sorting order, specifying up to four fields to sort by

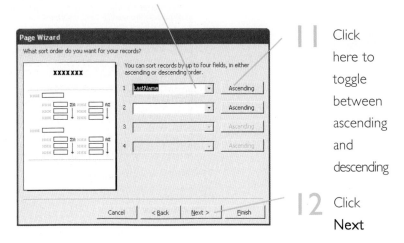

11 Click here to toggle between ascending and descending

12 Click **Next**

13 Give your new page a name

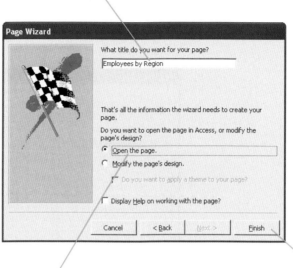

14 Tell Access what to do with your page after the wizard closes. You can specify a theme for your page here too, if you wish

15 Click **Finish**

16 Access creates your page. Click the plus sign (+) to see the detail and the minus (-) sign to collapse the view again

*To see how your web page will look in a browser, choose the **File > Web Page** Preview menu option.*

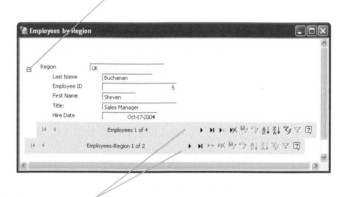

17 Use the navigation bars to move between records; add, edit and delete records and to sort and filter records, in exactly the same way as you do for forms

Creating a Page in Design View

You can create a page from scratch in the Design View. Just click on the **New** button on the Pages tab of the database window and select "Design view", or double click on the "Create form in Design view" link. The first method has the advantage that Access prompts you to choose a table or query upon which to base your page. Otherwise you'll have to specify it yourself in the page properties.

Components of the Page Design View

If you can't see the field list or toolbox, use the View menu options to display them.

Page Design Toolbar   Formatting (Page) Toolbar

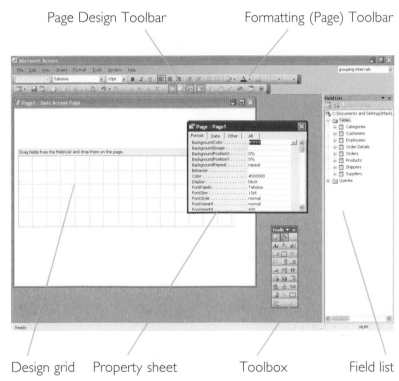

Design grid   Property sheet   Toolbox   Field list

The Page Design View gives you full control over the appearance and behavior of your data access page. The Toolbox is used to add various components to the page design grid. The Field List shows the structure of underlying tables and helps you quickly add data fields to your page. By setting different properties in the property sheet you can change the appearance and behavior of individual elements and the whole page.

Adding Fields and Controls

Adding Fields With the Field List

Access makes it easy to add data fields and other controls to your page in the Design view.

Page design has a lot in common with form and report design. See Chapters 6 and 8.

1   Double click the "Create data access page in Design view" link on the Pages pane of the Design view

2   Expand the field list by clicking the plus (+) symbol to the left of the Tables folder, just as you would in Windows Explorer. Navigate to the field you want to include in your page

If you don't see the field list or toolbox when you are in Design view, use the View menu options to display them.

3   Click on the field name and, holding down the left mouse button "drag" it across to the design grid. Release the mouse button to place the field

If you don't want to fire up your browser, click on the View button in the Page Design toolbar for a "snapshot" view of how your page will look.

4   Select the **File > Web Page Preview** menu item to see the page as it will appear in your browser. Use the navigation bar to move from record to record and observe how the field data changes as you do so.

Adding Controls With the Toolbox

Adding other items like labels, list boxes and combo boxes works in exactly the same way as for forms. Simply "drag" the desired item from the Control Box to the grid.

Moving and resizing controls is the same too. See Chapter 6 for further details.

Applying Themes

You can quickly change the overall appearance of your page using *themes.* Access ships with a selection of themes that combine backgrounds, fonts, bullets and other items that work well together. You can change the theme of your page at any time.

1 Open your form in Design view and select the **Format > Theme** menu option. A dialog box appears showing a list of available themes:

Click on the Set Default button to apply your chosen theme to ALL the pages in your database.

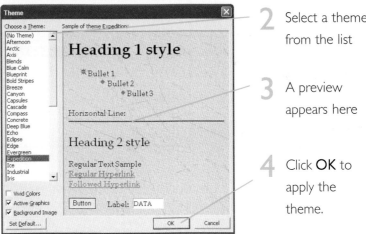

2 Select a theme from the list

3 A preview appears here

4 Click **OK** to apply the theme.

5 Click on the view button on the page design toolbar to see the effect!

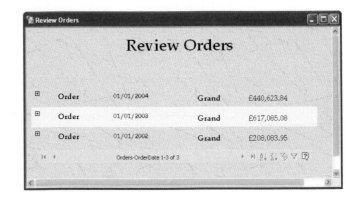

Using an Existing Web Page

Sometimes you'll already have a HTML document, maybe as part of an existing website and you want to use this format to present your data with. To create a data access page using an existing HTML document follow the steps below:

1 Double-click on the "Edit Web page that already exists" link in the Pages pane of the database window

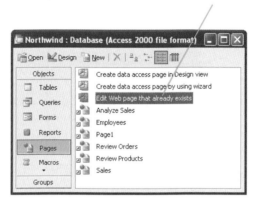

2 Find the HTML page you want to use and click **Open**

3 Access loads the page in design view

4 When you have finished making changes, save the page in the same folder as your database

Record Operations

Data Access Pages include by default a Record Navigation Bar. This is similar to the navigation bar for forms (see Chapter 6). You can use this bar to move from record to record as well as add, delete, sort and filter records.

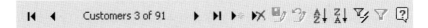

The Record Navigation Bar

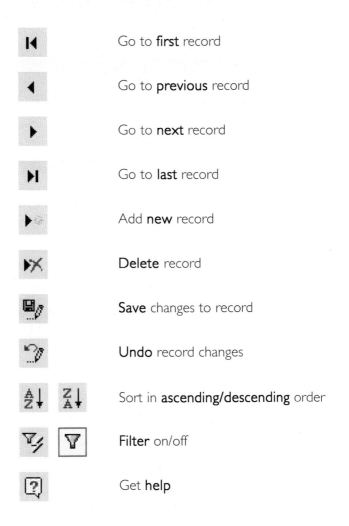	Go to **first** record
	Go to **previous** record
	Go to **next** record
	Go to **last** record
	Add **new** record
	Delete record
	Save changes to record
	Undo record changes
	Sort in **ascending/descending** order
	Filter on/off
	Get **help**

Protecting the Data

Customizing the Navigation Bar

You can choose to only show certain buttons on the navigation bar, or even omit it entirely. For example, a quick way to stop users from inadvertently deleting records is to remove the delete button!

1 Open the data access page in Design view and then select the navigation bar by clicking on it

2 Right click on the navigation bar and select the **Navigation Buttons** option

3 From the sub-menu, click on the delete item to deselect it

To reinstate the delete button (or any other button you removed from the toolbar), just put a check mark against it in the Navigation Buttons sub-menu.

4 When you run the page, the delete button is missing from the navigation bar

Protecting Individual Fields
You can also protect individual fields from being changed.

1. In Design view, select the data field you wish to make read-only by clicking on it

2. If you can't see the Properties window for the control, force it to display using the **View > Properties** menu option

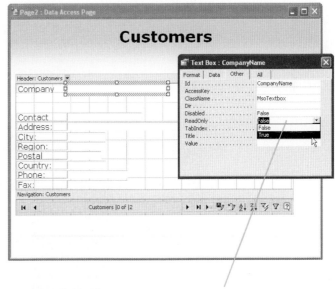

3. In the Other tab of the Properties window set the field's ReadOnly property to true

4. Click the **View** button on the toolbar and attempt to type something into that field – Access won't let you!

You can apply this change to several controls at once. Either: choose the **Edit > Select All** menu option to select all the controls on the page; "draw" a rectangle around the controls you want to include using the mouse cursor; or hold down the CTRL key while you click on controls. Then apply the property change.

Publishing and Printing

A web server hosts web pages and serves up HTML to your browser. HTML is the markup language that ensures that the information is displayed to you in the format intended by its author.

Publishing a Data Access Page

If you intend publishing your data access page on an intranet, then you may need to speak with your Network Administrator first. He or she will tell you which server location you can use to host your pages. If you wish to publish your page on the World Wide Web, you'll need to know the FTP address which should be supplied by your hosting provider.

1 With your page open in Design view, select the **File > Save As** menu option

2 In the Save Data Access Page box, type a name for your page in the "To" field

3 Navigate to Network Places and use the "Add Network Place" wizard to input the server details

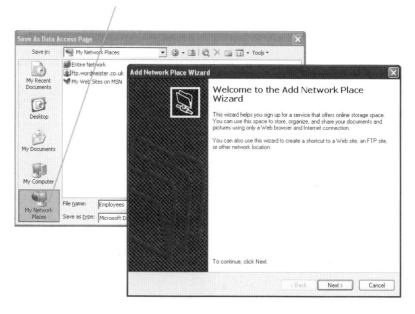

Printing a Data Access Page

To print a data access page either choose the **File > Print** menu option or click the **Print** button on the toolbar.

Finishing Touches

Now that you've got it up and running we're going to show you a few other things that you can do with your database to make it look like the work of a real pro! Among other things we'll show you how to add a switchboard and custom "splash" screen, keep your database secure, share your database with other users and carry out essential maintenance.

Covers

Chapter Ten

Creating a Switchboard

A switchboard is a type of form which gives your users access to all the functionality of your database. It's a page with buttons that link to the various forms, reports, etc. that you have created. In complex databases, some switchboard buttons can lead to other switchboards. If you've looked at the Northwind sample database you will have already seen a switchboard and the Database Wizard (which we saw in Chapter 2) includes a switchboard by default:

Main
switchboard
for the Asset
Tracking
database

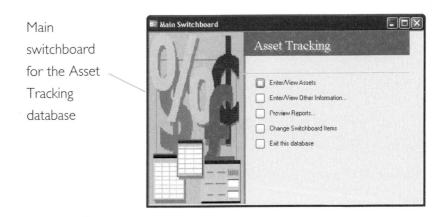

The Switchboard Manager

If you want to create your own switchboard (or modify one the wizard has built for you), you'll need to use the Switchboard Manager.

Select the **Tools > Database Utilities > Switchboard Manager** menu option

2   If you don't already have a switchboard, Access asks if you would like to create one – select "Yes"

3 The Switchboard Manager appears, with the main (default) switchboard ready for you to modify

If your database already contains switchboards, you'll see a list instead of the single default item shown here.

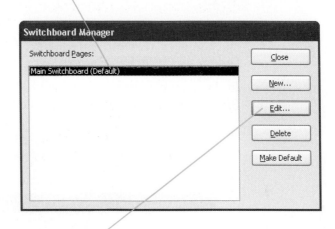

4 Click **Edit** to add items to the main switchboard

5 In the Edit Switchboard dialog, give your main switchboard a more descriptive name

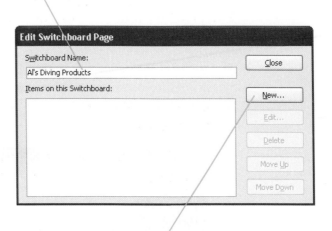

6 Click on **New** to add a new switchboard item

For each new switchboard item you add, you must define the following:

- The text you want to appear next to the button
- What you want to happen when the button is pressed
- (For some operations) which database object is involved

In this example, we're going to add a button that displays the Products form ready for the user to enter a new record:

1 Enter the text for the button

Not all actions in the "Command" list need to be associated with an object, "Exit Application" being one example. If Access requires an object it will prompt you for details.

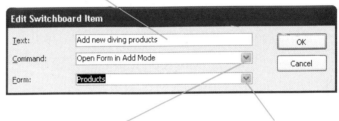

2 Choose an action from the drop-down list

3 Choose an object from the drop-down list (if appropriate)

4 Look in the Forms pane of the database window and you'll find a new Switchboard form. When you close and rerun the database, the switchboard will load automatically

5 Repeat steps 1-3 to add more items to your switchboard

Creating a Custom Splash Screen

The splash screen is the default graphic that displays while Access loads. The default splash screen looks like this:

If you really want your database to look professional, you can replace this graphic with one of your own. A quick way to do this is to use Paintshop Pro, Photoshop or any other graphics package you are familiar with. Create a Windows Bitmap file (.bmp) and save it with the same name and in the same folder as your Access database file. For example, if your database is called MyBusiness.mdb, your graphic will be called MyBusiness.bmp.

The Paint program that comes with Windows is good enough for simple splash graphics.

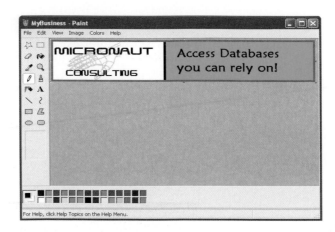

Now every time Access opens the MyBusiness database it opens your splash screen instead of the default one:

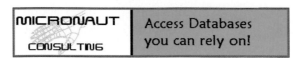

Creating a Startup Form

You can force Access to display a particular form when your database first starts. In this topic we're going to see how we can use a startup form to create a splash screen, which is preferable to the method we saw in the last topic.

In this example we are going to ensure that when we open our Camera Shop database, the first form we seem is the Products form:

1   Select the **Tools >**
     Startup menu option

2   Select the form you wish to display first from the drop-down list

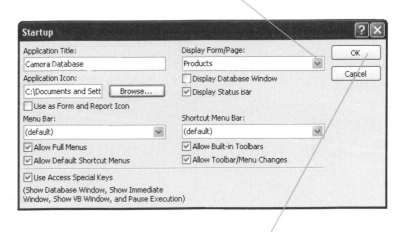

3   Click **OK,** close and then reopen the database and the form you
     selected will be loaded automatically

You can also specify other options in the startup dialog box, such as the name of the application, an icon to be associated with it and whether to hide the Database Window on startup.

If you elect to hide the Database Window on startup, you can bypass this by holding down the SHIFT key while clicking on the database you want to open.

Password Protecting the Database

A simple way of securing your database is to add password protection. To apply a password, you first need to open the database in a special way.

Access has a wealth of security options, including encryption of database contents and setting permissions for individual users. Consult Access Help.

1. Highlight the database you want to open by clicking on it

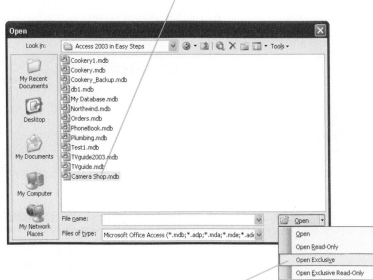

2. Click on the down arrow next to the **Open** button and choose "Open Exclusive"

3. Select the **Tools > Security > Set Database Password** option

4. Type the password, verify it by retyping it into the second box and then click **OK**

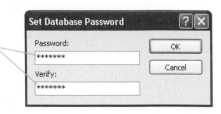

*Remove the password by using the **Tools > Security > Unset Database Password** menu option.*

5. Close the database, reopen it and this time you'll be prompted for the password that you just entered

Creating a MDE File

What is a MDE File?

If your database is used by other people, you might want to prevent them from inadvertently making changes that might break it. The easiest way to do this is to create a MDE file for them to use, while you keep the original MDB file hidden safely away somewhere.

In a MDE file, it is impossible to make any changes to forms, reports or VBA code (see Chapter 11). When you want to change something, you'll need to use the original .mdb file and then create a new .MDE file for your users.

Creating a MDE File

If you have stored data in the MDE file that is independent of your original MDB file, then you'll need to make a backup copy of the MDE file, create a new MDE file, delete its tables and then import them from the old MDE file.

1 Check that the database is in Access 2002/2003 format (on the Database window's title bar). If not, you will need to convert it

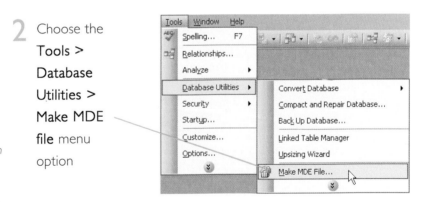

You will get an error if you try and create an MDE file from a database saved in Access 2000 format. See p. 20 for further information on file formats and instructions for converting to Access 2002-2003 format.

2 Choose the **Tools > Database Utilities > Make MDE file** menu option

3 Specify the folder and file name for the file and click **Save** on the toolbar

4 Ensure that your users use this MDE file and keep the original MDB file safe

Backing Up the Database

Backup your database regularly!

We've been stressing the importance of saving your creations, but you should back up the entire database on a regular basis too. If your file becomes corrupted or you have a hard disk crash, without a backup you'll lose all your data and tables, forms and other objects. A backup is a separate database file that contains all the information in the original at the point the backup is created.

If you have to restore your data from the backup copy, all the changes that you made to the original since that backup was taken will be lost. So make sure you schedule backups regularly.

1 Select the **File > Back Up Database** menu option

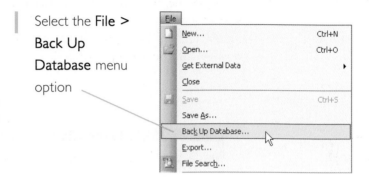

2 The Save dialog appears, with a suggested name for the backup file made up from the original file name and today's date. Either accept this name or enter a different one

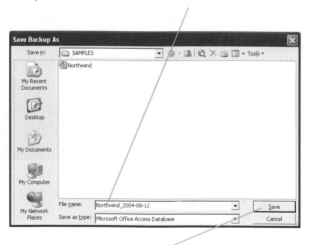

3 Click on the **Save** button to create a backup copy of your database

Compacting and Repairing

As well as backing up your database you should also compact and repair it regularly. Access databases have a habit of growing quite big and compacting can often reduce their size considerably. The repair operation helps remove any problems before they become an issue.

Also if you are working with a database and a serious problem occurs, Access will instruct you to compact and repair it. These are the steps you should take.

1   Using Windows Explorer, find your database file and make a note of the file size

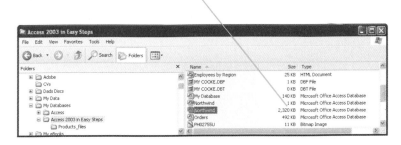

2   Select the **Tools > Database Utilities > Compact and Repair Database** menu option

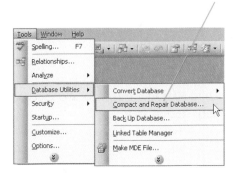

3   Access performs the necessary compaction and repair and then restarts the database. Check the file size. If you haven't compacted in a while it will be noticeably smaller

Macros

Macros are Access objects, just like Forms or Tables. Macros are the first step on the ladder towards programming and getting your Access application to do all the work!

Put simply, a macro is a set of actions that can all be run together, perhaps in response to some event. For instance, you might use a macro to open a particular form when the user presses a certain button, or run a sequence of reports instead of having to start each one manually.

Actions

Access supports a wide range of actions including opening forms and reports; moving from record to record from within a form; displaying messages to the user and filtering data. You can see a list of actions by clicking the **New** button in the Macros pane of the Database window, and then clicking in the Actions column.

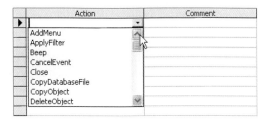

Arguments

Most macros require one or more *arguments* which tells Access how each action should be performed. For instance, to open a form, Access needs to know the name of the form. You can also specify certain conditions which have to be met before the action occurs. Action arguments are specified in the bottom half of the Macro design view.

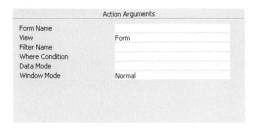

Creating a Macro

In this example we're going to create a macro that runs a report. In the next topic we will associate this macro with a button, so that when the user clicks the button, the report runs automatically.

1 Choose the OpenReport action from the drop-down list

2 Enter a comment, if you wish

All the "Open" actions: OpenReport, OpenForm, etc. work in a similar way. All you need to do is specify the name of the object you want the macro to open as an argument.

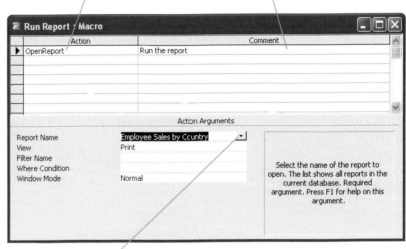

A quick way to create an action that opens a form, report or other object is to "drag" the object in question from the database window to the macro design view. Access creates a new open action automatically with the object as an argument.

3 In the Action Arguments section of the Macro Design View select a report

4 Save the macro by clicking the **Save** button on the toolbar

5 Click the **Run** button on the toolbar to test the macro

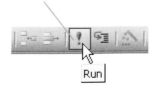

6 The macro launches the report

Specifying When to Launch the Macro

Having built our macro, we now need to tell Access how and when we want to run it. In this instance, we want Access to run the macro when the user clicks on the "Run Employees Report" button on our form.

Events

You can see which events are associated with a control by looking at that control's property sheet, on the Events tab.

All the controls on a form or report and even the objects themselves have a range of predefined events that Access can respond to. For example, our button control has an OnClick event which is triggered when the button is clicked, but also has many others such as when it gets the focus, loses the focus and so on. You can see all these events in the Event tab of the button's property sheet.

This makes Access enormously powerful, especially to programmers who can write program code to respond to these events (see Chapter 11). And we can use events to cause our macros to run when we want them to.

Attaching the Macro to the Button's OnClick Event

You can specify conditions so that the action only runs if the condition is met. See Access Help for further details.

| In the form design view, find the button's OnClick event in the property sheet Events tab

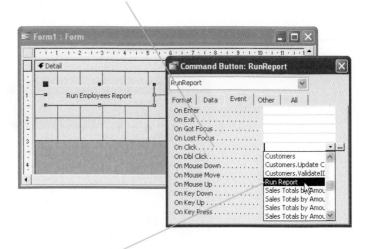

2 Select the macro to run when the button is clicked

3 Run the form, click the button and Access launches the macro

Creating Charts and Graphs

Charts and graphs are excellent means of presenting data in a visual format, making it easier for your users to understand and draw conclusions from.

With the Access Chart Wizard you can create a variety of sophisticated charts and graphs very easily. In this example, we want to create a bar graph of Road Traffic Accidents (RTA) occurring in a particular area. In our RTA table we have five fields: one for the year (Year) and four (Q1 - Q4) representing the number of accidents in each quarter.

If all the data you need is split across several tables, create a query that brings it all together and use that as the underlying data source for your chart.

Using the Chart Wizard

1. With the form or report which will contain the chart open in Design view, select the **Insert > Chart** menu option

2. Using the cursor, "draw" the boundaries of the chart on the form or report

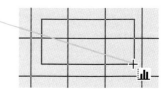

3. The Chart Wizard starts. Select the table or query where the chart will get its data from and click **Next**

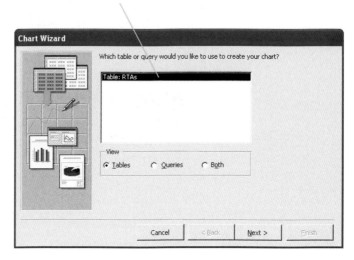

4 Use the arrows to select the fields you will include in the chart

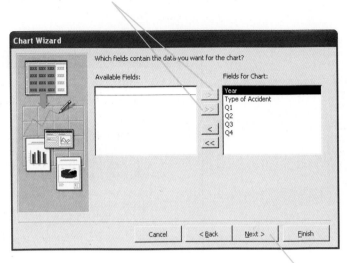

5 Click **Next**

6 Choose the type of chart you want to create

7 The panel explains each type of chart

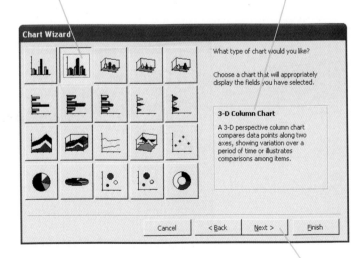

8 Click **Next**

9 "Drag" the fields from the list on the right onto the chart axes to change the layout of the report

When you drag a field to the Data area of the chart, Access assumes you want to summarize (i.e. add up) the data. If you double-click on a number field, you can choose a different way of handling the value.

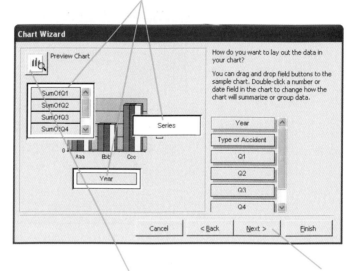

10 Click here for a preview of how your finished chart will look

11 Click **Next**

12 Choose a name for your chart

13 Click **Finish**

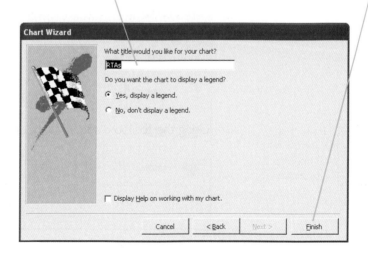

14 Run the form or report to see the finished chart

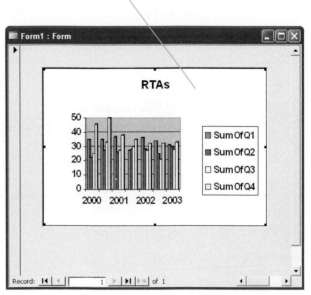

Adding a Chart to an Existing Form or Report

You can add a chart you have created in another form or report within the same database, or from a different database. To do so, you can either use cut and paste, or open the source object and destination object simultaneously and "drag" the chart from one to the other.

You can even include a chart or graph created in an entirely separate program. Follow these steps:

If you "link" to a chart created in another program, then any subsequent changes to that chart will be reflected in your database. If you "embed" the chart, then Access maintains a separate copy that is unaffected by changes to the original.

1 Using the toolbox, add an Unbound Object Frame control to the destination form or report

2 A dialog box appears. Select the "Create from file" option and click the Browse button to locate the chart

3 Put a check in the Link box if you want to link, rather than embed, this chart. Put a check in the "Display as Icon" box if you want to see an icon instead of the full chart and click OK

Modifying Charts and Graphs

When you use the Graph Wizard, Access actually launches another application in the background: Microsoft Graph. Graph creates the chart and places it into your form or report without you being any the wiser.

But if you need to make changes to your graphs or charts, you'll have to use Microsoft Graph directly.

Using Microsoft Graph

First open the object that contains the graph or chart in Design View. Then follow these steps:

You can type new values into the datasheet to see what effect it has on the graph.

1. Double-click anywhere in the chart area

2. Access launches Microsoft Graph where you can see the graph or chart with its underlying data

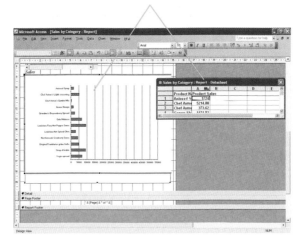

*Use the **View** > **Print Preview** menu option to see what your graph will look like without returning to Access.*

3. Using Graph's menus, make your changes. E.g. you can change the type of graph in the Chart menu, or the font in the Format menu

4. Click anywhere outside the graph to return to Access

Using the Table Analyzer

In Chapter 2 we stressed the importance of creating a set of related tables so that data is stored efficiently. Access provides a tool called the "Table Analyzer" that can look at the distribution of the data and make suggestions as to how it can be improved.

1 Select the **Tools > Analyze > Table** menu option

2 The first page of the wizard describes any problems it finds with your table organization and suggests ways to improve it

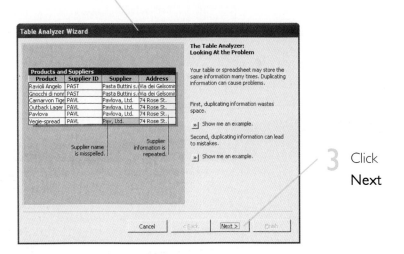

3 Click **Next**

4 The second page describes how Access plans to solve the issue by splitting tables so that each piece of data is stored in just one place. If you want to proceed click **Next**

5 In the next page of the wizard, select the table which contains the data that is being repeated and click **Next**

It's usually a good idea to at least review the suggestions made by the Table Analyzer.

6 Decide if you want the wizard to decide which fields go in which tables, or whether you would rather control this yourself

7 We'll assume here that you're going to ask the Table Analyzer for suggestions. Click **Next**

8 The next page shows the tables and relationship changes that the Table Analyzer suggests. Here it has moved the DeptManager, Building and DeptFax fields to a new table. To move fields back to the main table, simply drag them across. To create a new table not suggested by the wizard, drag a field to a blank area. The wizard displays a new table with a lookup to the existing one

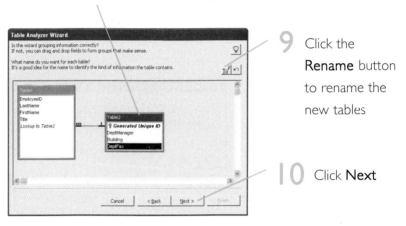

9 Click the **Rename** button to rename the new tables

10 Click **Next**

11 In the next page of the wizard, review any suggested changes to primary keys

12 Highlight a field and click on the Key button to make it the primary key:

13 To add a new field for a system-generated primary key, click here:

14 Click **Next** and decide whether to let Access create a query that looks like your original table. If you do, all forms, reports and other objects based on your existing table still work, while the database as a whole benefits from the changes the Table Analyzer has made

Using the Performance Analyzer

The Performance Analyzer considers individual objects in your database and suggests changes that can boost its overall performance.

1 Select the **Tools > Analyze > Performance** menu option

2 Select the tab which represents the objects you wish to optimize. Choose the "All Object Types" to see all objects at once

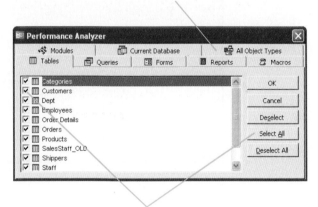

3 Put a check by the object(s) you wish to analyze, or click **Select All.** Then click **OK**

4 Access runs a check on all the objects you selected. Depending on the size of your database, this could take a little while

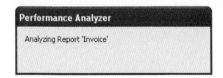

5 When Access has finished evaluating your database it displays the results. The results fall under three categories: **Recommendations, Suggestions** and **Ideas**

6 Click on one of the items in the list ...

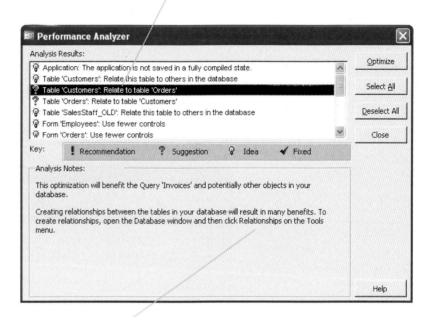

7 ... and Access displays additional explanations in the **Analysis Notes** pane

The Performance Analyzer is a useful tool, but common sense should always prevail. The Analyzer might pick up on something which you have designed that way for a very good reason.

8 If, after reading the explanation you wish to go ahead and let Access make the change, click on the **Optimize** button

9 Access then marks that item with a blue tick, signifying that it has been fixed

Taking It Further

We've covered the basic building blocks of an Access database as well as some of the more advanced features. If you've been following along then by now you are well on your way to becoming an expert Access user! But why stop there? Access has many other features that are too in-depth to cover in an introductory book like this. In this chapter we will give you an idea of what else Access is capable of should you wish to investigate further.

Covers

Chapter Eleven

Automating Access with VBA

By now you will have seen that Access is incredibly sophisticated, even "out of the box". So why would anyone want to learn programming?

Why Learn How To Program?

Well, in short, programming allows you to build intelligence into your applications and make them work the way *you* want them to. Access supports *Visual Basic for Applications* (VBA), which is a subset of their extremely powerful and popular *Visual Basic* programming language. Using VBA to automate Access 2003 you can:

- Let Access deal with complex, repetitive tasks and reduce human error

- Develop a solution that works the way you want it to

- Integrate Access with other Microsoft applications, including the rest of the Office suite and Internet Explorer

What is a Program?

Event-driven code tends to be stored along with the object where the event occurs.
Code that might be shared between several objects is usually put in a module.

A computer program is simply a list of instructions telling Access what needs to be done and in which order. The programming instructions we call *code*. Code can be associated with forms and reports or stored independently in the one object we haven't discussed yet: the *Module*.

Code is further divided into *procedures*, each of which contain a set of related instructions. These procedures can be called by other procedures within the program or associated with an *event* such as clicking on a button, or moving to a new record.

The Object Model

The "Object Model" gives every object in Access and other Microsoft applications that support automation a name that can be referred to from the program code. To control other applications using VBA, all you need to do is ensure that Access knows to refer to that application's object library. To "point" Access at the appropriate library you use the **Tools > References** menu option. The object model allows you to reference other Access objects (such as forms or reports) or an object in another application (e.g. a Microsoft Word document).

The Code Editor

To view code stored in a module, double-click on that module in the Database window. To view form or report code, select the **View > Code** menu option while the object is open in Design view.

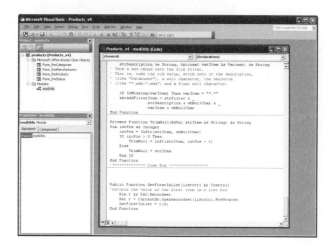

As well as giving you a place to create and edit code, the Code Editor has many other features including a debugging facility, syntax coloring and code completion.

Your First VBA Program

This is a trivial example of the capabilities of VBA, but it is designed to give you an idea of what to expect if you wish to explore the world of VBA programming yourself.

You can stop the wizards from displaying in the Design view by clicking the Control Wizards button in the toolbox.

We're going to design a form with a button and attach code to that button's OnClick event so that when the button is clicked a message is displayed showing the current date and time.

1. Create a new form in design view and add a command button. If the Button Wizard appears, cancel it

2. Give the button a meaningful name and caption in its property sheet

3 Right click on the button and choose the **Build Event** option from the sub-menu. In the "Choose Builder" dialog box select "Code Builder" and click OK

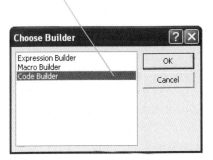

4 Access starts the code editor, loads the form code and creates a new, empty procedure in which to enter your own code

5 Enter the code exactly as it is shown here

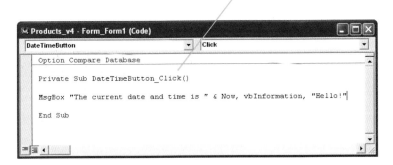

6 Save the form and run it. Click on the button and Access displays the system date and time

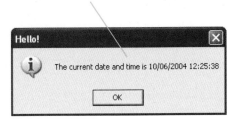

Learning XML

To learn more about XML see "XML In Easy Steps", written by Mike McGrath and published by Computer Step.

What is XML?

XML (Extensible Markup Language) is a standard way of encoding text and data for ease of processing and so that it can be exchanged across a broad range of hardware, operating systems and applications. As database developers, we like XML because it enables us to handle rich, complex data like multimedia, nested data or the complex documents we see on the Web.

Access 2003 and XML

Access 2003 offers improved support for XML. In particular it allows you to specify XSL (Extensible Stylesheet Language) transform files when importing data from or exporting data to XML format. This means that the transformation can be applied to the data before it is used to create a new table or append to an existing one.

Exporting XML

You can export any table, query, form or report to XML but in the case of a form or report it's the underlying data that gets exported. You can choose whether to export just the data, the schema, or both.

1 To export a complete object, select that object in the Database window and choose the **File > Export** menu option. If you only want to export certain records then open the object and select those records, or apply a filter to subset them

2 In the **Export** dialog box, specify a name and choose **XML** from the "Files of Type" dropdown box

3 Choose whether to export the data, the schema and/or presentation

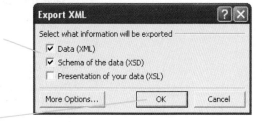

4 Click **OK**

Learning SQL

 For a detailed treatment of SQL see "SQL In Easy Steps", written by Mike McGrath and published by Computer Step.

SQL stands for *Standard Query Language* and is a powerful tool for working with data. The idea behind SQL was to provide a single set of commands that can be used to retrieve data from any type of database without having to learn each database's own particular query syntax.

Access uses SQL in queries, but hides the implementation behind the query builder interface to make it easier to use. So why would you want to learn SQL? Well, it's often easier to create or change an existing query by modifying its underlying SQL code than it is moving items around in the query grid. And, if you decide to learn VBA, you may wish to include SQL code in your programs.

Viewing SQL Generated By Access

To look at the SQL generated by a query, first open the query in Design View, then:

1 Click the **View** button on the toolbar

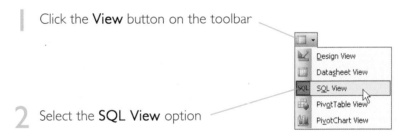

2 Select the **SQL View** option

3 Access displays the SQL code for the query

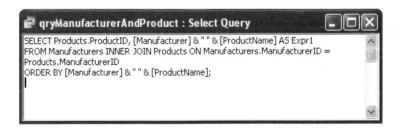

4 You can amend the SQL code directly in this window

Entering Your Own SQL

Just to give you an idea of what SQL is all about we're going to talk you through a simple SELECT query. The query will return a **data set** which is a collection of rows and columns containing the records and fields we specified in our SQL statement.

The simplest SQL statement consists of just two parts:

SELECT – This part consists of the SELECT keyword followed by the fields you want in the data set separated by commas. If you want to return all the fields in a table, type an asterisk (★) instead.

FROM – The FROM keyword followed by the table or tables from which the data should come.

The example below uses the Customers table in the Northwind sample database that ships with Access.

1 Create a new query in the Design View and when you're prompted to select a table, click **Cancel**

2 Click the SQL button on the toolbar

3 Enter the SQL exactly as it appears here

Take care to include the commas and the semicolon at the end, otherwise the SQL won't work.

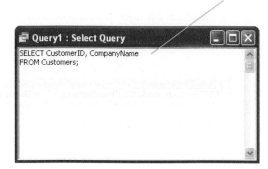

```
Query1 : Select Query
SELECT CustomerID, CompanyName
FROM Customers;
```

4 Click the **Run** button. Access displays a datasheet containing the fields and data you specified

Upsizing to SQL Server

Access is a powerful and robust database, capable of handling many thousands of records and being accessed by several users simultaneously. But if your requirements grow beyond that, Access makes it easy to upgrade to the vastly more powerful SQL Server.

Why SQL Server?

There are a number of reasons to consider upgrading to SQL server:

- **Performance and scalability** – SQL Server is generally faster than Access, processing queries in parallel using advanced multi-threading techniques. SQL Server databases can be measured in terabytes, whereas the upper limit for an Access database is 2Gb

- **Increased Availability** – SQL Server can be backed up while in use, which means that the database is available on a 24 hour basis

- **Tougher Security** – SQL Server makes the most of advanced operating system security features, as well as employing a few of its own

- **Server-side Processing of Queries** – By processing queries on the server and then sending the results back to the client, SQL Server can help keep network traffic at a minimum

Upsizing Methods

Depending on how you want to do it there are three main ways to upsize to SQL Server and Access has the Upsize Wizard to help you:

- **Upsize Everything** – Upsize every Access object from an Access Database file (MDB) to an Access Project File (ADP). The project file connects to the SQL Server database, thereby creating a client/server application

- **Just Upsize the Data** – Upsize the data or the data definitions.

- **Use Access as the Front-End** – Use Access as you normally do, but with all the "back-end" data residing on SQL Server. This is probably the easiest method, requiring few changes.

Index

D

E

F

M

macros
  actions 167
  arguments 167
  creating 168
  definition 22, 167
  launching 169
main screen 12
make-table query 111-112
many-to-many relationships 54, 60
MDB files 16
MDE files 164
memo (data type) 44
Microsoft Access 2003; see Access
Microsoft Excel 11, 63
Microsoft Graph 174
Microsoft Office 2003 11, 12, 14
Microsoft Office Online 14
Microsoft Word 11
modules 21-22, 180
moving and sizing handles 91, 127

N

navigation buttons 33, 79, 153-154
number (data type) 44
new file task pane 26
new records, adding; see Adding Records
Northwind sample database 19

O

object model; see Visual Basic for Applications
objects 21
observations 9; see also Records
Office assistant 14
OLE object (data type) 45
open file dialog box 16, 17
OnClick event 169
one-to-many relationship 25, 40, 54, 57
one-to-one relationship 25, 54, 57
OR queries 107
outer join 58

P

pages; see Data Access Pages
parent table 54
passwords; see Security
performance analyzer 177
pictures
  on forms 29
  on reports 135
primary key 25, 39, 48
printing
  data access pages 156
  reports 142
programming; see Visual Basic for Applications
properties
  for forms and their controls 89
  for reports and their controls 133
protecting data, within Data Access Pages 154

Q

Queries; see also Chapter 7
  action queries 21, 112
  adding fields 110
  AND queries 108
  append queries 115
  creating
    in design view 102-103
    using wizard 100-101
  definition 21
  delete queries 113
  deleting fields 110
  displaying results of 109
  duplicate records 116
  hiding fields in 109
  make-table queries 111-112
  OR queries 107
  removing fields 110
  select queries 100
  sorting results 109
  special queries
    find duplicate records wizard 116
    find unmatched records wizard 116
  unmatched records 116
  update queries 114
  using to find records 104-108
    exact matches 104
    multiple criteria 107
    multiple data sources 106
    multiple fields 108
    range of matches 105

R

fixed width 66, 68
themes, for data access pages 151
toolbars 13
toolbox 93, 130, 132, 150
tooltips 13
totals, on reports 140
transform files, XML 183

XML 183
XSL 183

unbound controls 85
unmatched records 116
update queries 114
URLs 45
user requirements 24

yes/no (data type) 45

validation
    field level 51
    record level 52
    Rule (field property) 47
    text 47
VBA; see Visual Basic for Applications
viewing records
    in the datasheet 33
    in forms 78
Visual Basic for Applications 22, 180

web pages 152
wildcards 36
Wizards
    data access page 146-148
    database 26-29
    form 72-73
    import 63
    list and combo box 93-96
    query 100-101, 116
    report 118-122
    table 38-41